"This small handbook is precisely what every beginning theology student needs to write a coherent, well-argued, properly researched essay. Mike Kibbe is not only a master teacher (his instructional style is evident throughout) but he is a master researcher (whose recent PhD demonstrates his fresh skills). Let Kibbe become your coach and encourager. If you do, you'll find guidance for how to organize that winning research project. You'll find lists of common errors that countless students make. But above all, you'll discover a gold mine of wisdom that I wish we could put into the hands of every student who sets out to write a paper."

Gary M. Burge, Wheaton College

"Mike Kibbe's guide for writing research papers is an excellent resource for both college and graduate level students. Its compact size belies its wealth of helpful advice and information. The step-by-step instruction should give students confidence, while pointing out pitfalls and offering examples from the author's own experience. There are many time-saving suggestions that will make research and writing efficient without compromising integrity. And the tone is conversational, as if Kibbe is having a one-on-one conversation with the reader. This book is essential for students who write research papers . . . and for professors who want to *enjoy* reading what their students produce."

Dennis Okholm, professor of theology, Azusa Pacific University

"Kibbe's *From Topic to* ~~Th~~ ~~~~ ~~~~ concise but complete course in the art and scienc ~~~~ g, complete with five sh ~~~~ d, gather, understand, ~~~~ e

D1430294

assembly instructions for things like bookshelves, Kibbe's directions are easy to follow, providing everything one needs to know to write and sustain a theological thesis (except the theology). I said 'thesis' and not 'topic' because Kibbe encourages me not to confuse them (a topic is a subject area; a thesis is a specific claim about that area). This is only one of the many practical bits of wisdom readers will find herein."

Kevin J. Vanhoozer, Trinity Evangelical Divinity School

"Michael Kibbe's compact guide delivers a lot of practical wisdom for those beginning to write theological research papers. Other guides can be so long that assigning them competes with the actual reading and writing you want students to undertake! By contrast, this one gets to the point and gives concrete examples without denying the mysteries of the research process."

Daniel J. Treier, Wheaton College

FROM TOPIC TO THESIS

A GUIDE TO THEOLOGICAL RESEARCH

MICHAEL KIBBE

IVP Academic

An imprint of InterVarsity Press
Downers Grove, Illinois

InterVarsity Press
P.O. Box 1400, Downers Grove, IL 60515-1426
ivpress.com
email@ivpress.com

©2016 by Michael Kibbe

*InterVarsity Press® is the book-publishing division of InterVarsity Christian
Fellowship/USA®, a movement of students and faculty active on campus at
hundreds of universities, colleges and schools of nursing in the United States of
America, and a member movement of the International Fellowship of Evangelical
Students. For information about local and regional activities, visit intervarsity.org.*

Cover design: Cindy Kiple
Interior design: Beth McGill
Images: Katie Edwards/Getty Images

ISBN 978-0-8308-5131-7 (print)
ISBN 978-0-8308-9981-4 (digital)

Printed in the United States of America ⊗

Library of Congress Cataloging-in-Publication Data

Names: Kibbe, Michael, 1980-
Title: From topic to thesis : a guide to theological research / Michael Kibbe.
*Description: Downers Grove : InterVarsity Press, 2016. | Includes bibliographical
references and index. | Description based on print version record and CIP data
provided by publisher; resource not viewed.*
*Identifiers: LCCN 2015042607 (print) | LCCN 2015040193 (ebook) | ISBN
9780830899814 (eBook) | ISBN 9780830851317 (pbk. : alk. paper)*
Subjects: LCSH: Theology--Research. | Theology--Authorship. | Academic writing.
*Classification: LCC BR118 (print) | LCC BR118 .K53 2016 (ebook) | DDC
230.072--dc23*
LC record available at http://lccn.loc.gov/2015042607

P	18	17	16	15	14	13	12	11	10	9	8	7	6	5	4	3	2
Y	30	29	28	27	26	25	24	23	22	21	20	19	18	17			

To Sue Park-Hur,

for giving me the chance to try out my ideas

about theological research on unsuspecting

students at the Fuller Theological

Seminary Writing Center.

CONTENTS

ACKNOWLEDGMENTS

THIS BOOK BEGAN AS a two-hour workshop for the Writing Center at Fuller Theological Seminary in 2009, and thanks are due to Sue Park-Hur, then director of the Writing Center, for allowing me to hone my ideas in that context. Courtney Bacon, a PhD student at Fuller, used the earliest written drafts of the material as required reading in her Orientation to Theological Studies courses, and her feedback alongside that of David Downs and Rich Erickson of Fuller Seminary brought the manuscript to adolescence. Credit for later revisions and additions is due especially to two Wheaton College mentor-colleagues: Michael Graves (for his encyclopedic knowledge of ancient texts and modern editions) and Daniel Treier (for his insights into how a book like this one might actually be used in undergraduate and graduate contexts). And thanks are due, finally, to David Congdon and the IVP editorial staff for bringing the project to completion.

INTRODUCTION

HOME DEPOT RECENTLY RAN a commercial depicting a man standing in his living room staring admiringly at the ceiling fan he had just installed, wondering why he held in his hand one last bolt that seemed like it should have played some part in the assembly. In the next scene, the ceiling fan comes crashing down onto the glass coffee table placed inexplicably beneath it, followed by another crash as the man throws the fan through his living room window in frustration. The point of the commercial is that you can save yourself a lot of trouble if you just pay a little bit extra and have the experts at Home Depot do the work for you. Of course, the point might also have been that if the man had read the instructions a little more carefully, none of this would have happened.

You've been there, haven't you? You bring home a new piece of furniture—let's say a new desk (less intimidating than a ceiling fan, perhaps)—and those two terrifying words appear: "Assembly required." You have three options:

(A) Call the experts and stave off any chance of disaster. Under certain circumstances—you can wait a week for them to come out, you can afford to pay the extra fees, you aren't motivated to learn how to do it yourself—this can work. (B) Wing it. Dump all the pieces on the floor and start putting things together that look like they go together. This too can work under certain circumstances—you assemble furniture for a living, the desk has only three pieces, or you have a surplus of time in which to conduct trial-and-error. (C) Read the instructions and follow them. You already know I prefer this one!

This book is designed to be an instruction manual for "assembling" your theological research paper. Option A doesn't work. You can't just call in the experts—*you* have to write the paper. Why do you have to write the paper and do so in such a way that the thoughts and arguments in the paper are yours and not a regurgitation of someone else's? Because if you are taking a course that requires a theological research paper, part of the purpose of that course is *skill development*. Doing research develops several skills: the skill of *finding* information, the skill of *processing* (reading, understanding, correlating, evaluating) information and the skill of *communicating* information. Calling in the experts is antithetical to skill development, so that just won't do.

Option B also doesn't work, at least not within the parameters you have for your research project. You could spend countless hours perusing the library stacks, hoping to stumble across the right books for your paper. But I'd be willing to bet that you don't have "countless hours"! More than likely, you've got a couple of weeks to write three large papers and four small papers, give two presentations, and prepare for a comprehensive exam in at least one ancient language—and all this while working part-time, volunteering at your church part-time, and spending time with your family somewhere in there. So sure, if you walk the library aisles long enough, you might find something. Or if you simply google your research topic, you might turn up something useful. But where do you find the criteria by which you judge something to be "useful," and how much time are you willing to spend scrolling through page after page of useless hits until you find something that meets those criteria? Time is a valuable commodity, and this option is guaranteed to waste a lot of it.

And so we are left with Option C: read the instructions—this book! Like an instruction manual, this book is designed to be as short as possible—complete step one, step two, etc., then stand back and admire your finished product. Theological research isn't *quite* as simple as assembling a piece of furniture, but the basic idea is the same: take certain steps involving *these* pieces and not *those* pieces, in *this* order and not *that* order, and when you're done you'll have a product you can be proud of. And hopefully, your story won't end with you throwing a pile of books through your window!

THE PROCESS: FROM "TOPIC" TO "THESIS"

Like an instruction manual, this book will be most profitable if you begin by skimming through the whole thing
to get your bearings and see the broad strokes of where it
will be leading you. Once you have done that, return to the
first chapter and, following the instructions, begin your
research. This book is not a reference book that you should
pull off the shelf to address a variety of topics at a variety
of isolated points within the research process, with the
exception of some of the appendixes.[1] Rather, it is a simple
book designed to take you step by step from a research
topic to a research *thesis*.

Every research paper begins with a topic, usually one
specified in your course syllabus. The amount of direction
you receive on your initial topic will vary from class to
class. One professor will require you to write on a topic
that falls broadly within the scope of the course: "Write an
8–10 page research paper on some aspect of Christology."
Christology, then, is your initial topic. Another professor
will give you a more specific topic as a starting point:
"Write a 2,500-word research paper on the kingdom of
God in Mark's Gospel." This initial topic is narrower than
"Christology," for instance, but is still fairly broad. Usually,
a text of Scripture will be the most specific topic you will
be assigned: "Write a 10–12 page exegetical paper on Isaiah

---

[1]See appendix B for a list of reference works that are useful in this way.

6:1-9," or "Write a 2,000-word research paper on one of the prophetic call narratives."

Do not make the mistake of moving immediately from topic to paper. A research paper is not built around a topic, but a *thesis*. A *topic* is a set of information that concerns a specific thing, such as Christology, the kingdom of God in Mark's Gospel or prophetic call narratives. A *thesis* is a specific claim you make about that particular set of information. The research process is the movement you make from *identifying* that set of information (your topic), to making an *argument* about that set of information (your thesis). Your paper will not merely be "about Christology" but will make a specific claim about a particular issue within Christology.

Think of it this way: in speech class in high school or college, you probably gave both informative speeches and persuasive speeches. In informative speeches, you were taught to say "In this speech I will inform you about . . ." or "My topic for this speech is . . ." But in persuasive speeches you said "In this speech I will attempt to argue that . . ." or "My goal in this speech is to persuade you that . . ." The key is that *every research paper is like a persuasive speech.* You must always make some kind of argument, and that argument is called your *thesis.*

The question is, how do you go from focusing on a subject to focusing on an argument? In other words, how do you get from topic to thesis? The goal of this book is to teach you exactly that.

THE ONGOING CONVERSATION

Before we dive into the nuts and bolts of theological research, you might want to know a bit about its history. This book will occasionally describe research as analogous to entering an ongoing conversation—if that analogy works, you might want to know a few things not only about what is being discussed, but who is discussing it. A conversation is necessarily a group activity, and the better you know the people around you, the better prepared you will be to converse with them.

Theological research is a multitiered process. In many cases, for example, your theological research will involve reading the Bible. But to read the Bible is to be dependent on a community of others who have done a great deal of work to make that reading possible: archaeologists discovering manuscripts (copies of one biblical text or another), papyrologists analyzing and typesetting those manuscripts, textual critics examining variant readings in those manuscripts and rendering judgment on which option is the best one, and translators taking the resulting Greek or Hebrew or Aramaic text and rendering it into English (or another language) that is appropriate for the kind of Bible they are trying to produce—the one you plan to use in your theological research.[2]

---

[2]For sources written since the invention of the printing press, the process is obviously not so complicated. But even then we are often dependent on transcription (lecture notes recorded by the students

Of course, your dependence on others does not stop with the formation of the biblical text you're currently using. Theological research is not, nor has it ever been, a solo act. Whether you are thinking about theological research for the very first time or you have written more books than most people will ever read, you are and always will be dependent on the work of others.

Who are those others? Well, theological research has been taking place for a long time. People have been reading and analyzing the Bible for as long as there have been pieces of the Bible to read and analyze; in fact, it is quite common for later portions of Scripture to serve as guides toward understanding earlier portions (and vice versa—but that's another conversation!). The research conversation, in other words, begins within the Bible itself. After the time of the apostles, that conversation really takes off. From the early centuries of the church we have letters, sermons, commentaries, creeds and other written sources. Sources multiply exponentially in the medieval and early modern eras, particularly with the advent of the university and (later) the printing press, and in the digital era there is so much scholarship being produced that we have entire journals dedicated to surveying and synthesizing recent trends.

---

of some scholar) or translation (as I discuss below, a great deal of theological research has been done by those whose native tongue is not English).

This mass of possible conversation partners can be overwhelming in several different ways. First, you won't have to read many premodern sources before you realize just how different the conversation was in the fifth century (for example) compared with the conversation today. You might read Theodoret's commentary on Exodus and wonder if he's even talking about the same Exodus! If that literature is to be helpful, you'll often have to take the extra step of translating their answers to *their* questions into meaningful answers to *our* questions. Of course, you might eventually find that Theodoret sees Exodus more clearly than more recent scholars do—but that takes time and energy you might not have between now and when your paper is due.

Second, in both the first century and the twenty-first century, a lot of potential conversation partners aren't speaking your language. Literally. Early Christian literature was written primarily in Greek, Latin, Coptic and Syriac. Only in the last couple of centuries has English become a major theological research language, and even now serious scholarship requires facility in German and French. If you are really ambitious, you might want to pick up Italian, Dutch and Spanish as well. Oh, and if you want to do Old Testament studies in particular, get ready not only for Hebrew and Aramaic, but also for Ugaritic, Akkadian and a host of other Semitic languages that form the linguistic milieu of ancient Israel. The good news, of course, is that the Bible, whether the Hebrew or Aramaic or Greek or Samaritan versions of it, has been translated into English. But a lot of literature about the Bible hasn't, and that literature about the Bible is, in theory, your conversation partner.

Third, deciphering which versions of whose translation are the right ones for you can be as intimidating as reading sources written in another language. Just go to Amazon .com and see how many different editions of Augustine's *Confessions* or Plato's *Republic* you can find—you'll see what I mean. These texts were not originally written in English, so the version you are going to read was translated by someone, and you probably know from all the hubbub over English Bible translations that no two translators think exactly alike. On this particular issue, there's an easy solution: ask your professor. More often than not, they will be able to point you to their preferred version or translation rather quickly.

To some degree, these first three problems only appear if you go looking for them. Your first foray into the literature is probably going to reveal modern books and articles that only exist in one version, and that version is written in English. In many cases, this is okay—your Gospels professor does not expect you to learn Latin just so you can read medieval homilies on the transfiguration, nor does your Reformation theology professor assume that you can figure out which version of Calvin's *Institutes* you should be reading—if they care, they'll tell you! A fourth problem, though, is inescapable: there is simply too much to read, even if we limit our conversation partners to English sources written in the last few decades. There is just no way around it. Consider this: one of my favorite websites, polumeros.blogspot.com (a resource for scholarship on the book of Hebrews), currently lists eighteen *English* commentaries on Hebrews coming out in the next few years. Or this: by my count there were around one hundred and fifty scholarly sources (commentaries, journal articles, essays and books) on Hebrews published between 2010 and 2015. That's one book of the Bible (and not the most widely written-on book in the Bible, not by a long shot) in a five-year period. This, of course, is one of the major reasons why you are reading this book! You need some way to get to the *right* sources in a reasonable amount of time so that you can be a participant in this very long, very diverse and very exhilarating conversation.

So there's good news and bad news concerning the history of the theological research conversation. The bad news is that the conversation is far more complex than you imagined. The good news is that it is possible to get enough familiarity with that conversation to make a meaningful contribution to it (in the form of a quality research paper) within a reasonable amount of time (i.e., by the time your paper is due!).

THEOLOGICAL RESEARCH IS LIKE ANY OTHER KIND OF RESEARCH

It has long been axiomatic among biblical scholars that we should read the Bible like any other book. Scripture, many suggest, is not exempt from the rules that apply to proper interpretation of any other human-authored text: it follows the usual rules of grammar, linguistics, historical contexts and so on. In other words, whatever principle of interpretation is appropriate for reading Shakespeare applies equally to Scripture—the fact that one claims divine inspiration and authority in the Christian community is of little or no consequence for one's hermeneutical method.

This notion has a great many possible entailments— some of which (in my view) are valid, and some of which (in my view) are not. This book isn't about hermeneutics, at least not centrally, so I won't take you down all those rabbit holes! But regarding *research*, the axiom points to something important: the theological research process is very similar to other research processes, particularly those involving *texts* as one's subject matter.

Every research process has a preparation component, a field component and an analysis component. You might imagine biological research as primarily about a white-clad figure hunched over a microscope in a lab, examining specimens, but where do the specimens originate? How are they stored prior to examination? Then, after they have been observed under the microscope, how are the results of those observations recorded and analyzed? Ethnographers, similarly, spend a portion of their time conducting personal interviews, but then they listen to recordings of those interviews, enter data into specialized software programs (which had to be designed by someone familiar with ethnography) and so on. And, of course, the quality of the results of ethnographic research is directly related to the quality of the questions asked in the interview—questions prepared in advance.

Theological research goes through similar phases. As I mentioned in the previous section, someone has to discover, protect, decipher, transcribe and translate the subjects of our research long before we find them on the library shelf. This, we might say, includes both the preparation and field components of the process. However, this book is focused on the analysis portion of the task: the part that, like it or not, involves going to the library and reading. And reading. And reading some more. If that sounds thrilling to you, I can relate! If that sounds like torture to you, I hope the process described in this book will relieve your angst.

From another angle, you are in the preparation stage of your research: gaining tools and insights (including those in this book) that you will bring to every research project from this point forward. You also spend the first few weeks of every semester in the preparation stage of that course:

learning the ropes of a new area of study without which you could not write a research paper. Then you'll do your fieldwork as you gather sources and create your research bibliography (I'll explain these steps later in the book). Finally, you'll do your analysis: print, read, underline, highlight, think, compare, critique, etc.

Like the research process described above, the goal of theological research is in a broad sense not so different from that of any other kind of research. Put simply, the goal of any kind of research is *new knowledge*. Big surprise, I know! But what may not be so obvious is *to whom* this knowledge is new. When we see headlines like "Groundbreaking Research Suggests . . ." in various digital and print media forms, we assume that researchers have obtained knowledge that is new for *everyone*. This is seldom the case, especially in the theological disciplines, but words like *groundbreaking* grab our attention and create the impression that we will be missing something new and extremely important if we do not read the article or buy the product.[3] But here's something for you to remember: the

---

[3]A great example of this is the recent "provocative" and "meticulously researched" book by Reza Aslan called *Zealot: The Life and Times of Jesus of Nazareth* (New York: Random House, 2013), which "sheds new light" on Jesus by describing him as, primarily, a zealous opponent of imperial powers (quotes drawn from the publisher's blurb). Larry Hurtado, emeritus professor of New Testament and Early Christianity at the University of Edinburgh, describes this claim about Jesus (and Aslan's attempt at rehashing it) as one of many "zombie claims" that appear on occasion in mainstream

goal of your research is not to present knowledge that you think is new to *everyone else*. You haven't had time—as I hope the previous section on the history of theological research makes clear—to know if what you have concluded from your research is new to anyone else or not. So don't worry about that! In fact, I strongly urge you not to use "Is this new/provocative/groundbreaking/sensational?" as a guiding principle at any point in your research process. Rather, the goal of your research is new knowledge for *you*. You, and you only. No one else.[4] This is true across the academic disciplines (What are the odds you'll find something in that frog that your biology lab instructor hasn't seen before?), but it bears special mention here. This will eventually change if you pursue theological research long-term. My dissertation examination committee, for example, asked me what significant original contribution I thought I had made to my subdiscipline (the epistle to the Hebrews)—but this is not a question you should be worrying about at this stage of things.

---

media thanks to nonexperts trying to make a buck through provocative and clearly underresearched ideas, despite the fact that those ideas have been put to death over and over by scholars who do actual research. You can read Hurtado's comments in full here: larryhurtado.wordpress.com/2013/08/15/zombie-claims-and-jesus-the-zealot.

[4]This doesn't mean your professor will never learn anything from your papers—I learn things from my students' papers all the time. If it happens, great! But your goal, as a student, is not to come up with something your professor hasn't seen before.

One final thought: we may be tempted to think that there is a subjectivity to theological research that we would never bring, for example, to the sciences. Fields like mathematics, chemistry, geology and the like—these, we think, are concrete and objective. (Have you ever heard someone in a chemistry lab say, "I feel like this is what it means to me"?) But theological research and biological research are essentially the same at this level: a researcher examines a research subject in order to be taught by that subject. What will you learn from what you see through the lens of your microscope? What will the book lying open on your desk teach you? The thing you are studying (a cross section of a leaf or the Gospel of Matthew) and your specific point of interest (plant cellular structure or triplets in the Sermon on the Mount) may vary, but the basic idea remains the same. Both tasks require focus, humility, time and a specific skill set—a skill set that, in the case of theological research, I hope you will more fully possess when you have finished reading this book.

THEOLOGICAL RESEARCH IS *NOT* LIKE ANY OTHER KIND OF RESEARCH

The previous section may prompt the rejoinder, "Isn't theological research different because its research subject is *God*?!"[5] Doesn't that somehow make theological research

---

[5]Notice the word *subject* here. It is an odd but revealing feature of how the English language functions in the academy today that we can refer to both a research "object" and a research "subject" and have

a different activity from other kinds of research? Well, no and yes.

The difference between theological research and other kinds is *not*, first of all, that it is a "spiritual" or "sacred" activity whereas researching US history, molecular biology and Shakespeare are "secular" activities. No research process, theological or otherwise, could ever be purely secular—not if every research subject is either Creator or creation, and if to research creation properly is to learn something about the Creator. The distinction between theological research and other sorts of research cannot fall along sacred/secular lines. To put it another way, theological research is a spiritual undertaking not because it is *theological* research, but because it is theological *research*— one attempt among many to understand more fully the Creator and his creation.

One feature of theological research that is like other kinds in general but different in the particulars has to do with our embodiment of the topic. Great research always involves closeness, involvement, vulnerability—the willingness to get your hands dirty by investing yourself in ways that go beyond studying extra hard or reading extra

---

precisely the same referent in mind. I use the word *subject* because it implies active participation in the process—a subject does things, while an object has things done to it. That which we study speaks to us and shapes us; it does not merely lie passively on the desk while we examine it.

carefully. Want to know about predators in Saharan Africa? Get ready to spend some time around predators in Saharan Africa. Books will only get you so far. Knowledge does not exist at a distance—you have to get dirty. In theological research, this means many things, of which I will mention three.

First, since your research subject is God, theological research is necessarily an act of confession—confession that you do not deserve to know God, confession that you are human and therefore limited in your ability to understand him, confession that you are sinful and therefore limited in your ability to know your own limitations.

Second, theological research has an ever-present subject-matter expert—the Holy Spirit—who guides us into all truth. Asking the Spirit for wisdom is not a replacement for typical research activities (reading, analyzing, etc.); rather, we listen to the Spirit *while* listening to those who have already asked him the very same questions we are now asking. We need those others in the listening community because they are often better listeners than us!

Third, the problem with theological research is that God is actually unknowable to us unless he graciously makes that knowledge available to us (an act we call God's *self-revelation*). The supreme act of that self-revelation took place in the God-man Jesus Christ, and so the ultimate answer to the question "How do we do theological research?" will always come back to him.

How is that relevant to theological research method? Once again, there are huge hermeneutical questions I won't answer here! But I'll say this much: to know God we must know Christ, to know Christ we must imitate him, and to imitate Christ we must (especially) become like him in his death and resurrection. To do theological research, which has as its end the knowledge of God, therefore requires (among other things) participation in the dying and rising of Jesus. This has innumerable applications, but it must at least mean that we enter into the theological research process in order to serve the church rather than advance our own careers, and that we treat our fellow researchers as fellow servants rather than fellow competitors for grades, grants, jobs and the like. To use the knowledge of God for selfish gain is to deny that we have any true knowledge of God in the first place, if indeed God has supremely revealed himself in Christ, who humbled himself.

Two other features of theological research that are different (quantitatively if not qualitatively) from other kinds are worth mentioning. First, there is a difference of authority. The subject of theological research is itself subject to no higher authority—we do not come to conclusions about what God has said and then decide whether or not we agree with him. In contrast, we ought to read someone like Nietzsche carefully, humbly and prayerfully, but also critically—Nietzsche himself does not offer the last word.

This difference of authority changes my research

posture in dramatic ways. I respect Nietzsche; I worship God. I listen carefully to Nietzsche in order to treat him with the dignity worthy of one made in God's image. But I listen carefully to God in order to treat him as the sovereign ruler of the universe who speaks that universe, including his image bearers who inhabit it, into existence.

This posture toward God's authority points to a second unique feature of theological research: *consequences*. All research-based decisions have consequences: buying a Hummer because the website you read said Hummers get great fuel mileage will have financial consequences, and going on the all-cheese diet because a friend said, "It worked for me" will have health consequences. In terms of academic, text-based research, misreading Dickens might lead to wrong beliefs about nineteenth-century England, about Dickens's characters or about Dickens himself. But the difference between misreading Dickens and misreading Scripture is that when it comes to how your life is shaped by your research, the greater authority granted to Scripture makes it less likely that you'll head off faulty decisions based on that research. That is, we may believe that we have rightly understood Dickens, but there is another line of defense (Scripture) that may keep us from basing our lives on that interpretation of Dickens. We might think, rightly or wrongly, that Dickens calls us to certain actions, and yet still say, *Hang on, that can't be right—look at Scripture!* But if our understanding of Scripture goes awry, we won't be able to say, *Hang on, that can't be right—look at Dickens!*

Similarly, I can place appropriate boundaries around the shaping effects of certain kinds of research on my life. I may find Bertrand Russell compelling in any number of ways, but there are pieces of my life from which I can appropriately bracket him out. Not so for God! No activity—whether intellectual or physical or relational or any other kind—is exempt from the shaping effects of my view of God. The one thing theological research *cannot* be, therefore, is a purely academic exercise or one limited to certain spheres of my existence and kept away from others. To do theological research is to think about the whole of one's life, not just a piece of it.

In the end, though, the simple affirmation that theological research is about *knowing God* is enough. I do not mean that the only way to know God is to go to graduate school and read books about him in the library all day. But I do mean that when we learn about God, we either learn what is false about God or what is true about him. It is enough to say that we are in pursuit of true beliefs about God. That pursuit needs no further justification, for as God exists in himself and has no external cause or higher purpose (that is, God doesn't exist for some purpose beyond himself, as everything else does), so knowing God does not *need* to be justified by how that knowledge shapes my life, or the world around me. Research aimed immediately at *creation* requires some further justification, whether improvement of living conditions, financial benefit, subsequent knowledge of God or some other perceived good. Research aimed immediately at the *Creator* requires no such justification; knowledge of God—the only appropriate end of theological research—is a good in itself.

DEFINING KEY TERMS

Instruction manuals usually come with a key, a list of symbols that correspond to the various pieces you will be using to assemble your project (e.g., AA = 2" black Phillips-head screws; D = 12" × 24" × 1" board). Without the key, it is nearly impossible to understand what the manual is asking you to do at each phase of the assembly process. In the same way, there are some terms you will need to be familiar with before you can begin your research.

Theological. The most important term of all! If you're reading this book, you probably didn't think twice about this word—you assume you already know what it means. I am not going to say all that could be said about what it means for anything, even research, to be "theological," but you do need a little bit of clarity about the term *theological* and what it suggests I am and am not going to do in this book.

In the academy, the word *theological* is sometimes juxtaposed with *biblical* to point to a disciplinary distinction. The course you are taking that requires a research paper may be either a biblical studies course (Old Testament or

New Testament) or a theological studies course (systematic theology or historical theology). Moody Bible Institute, where I currently teach, has both a Department of Bible and a Department of Theology. Wheaton College, my former institution, has a Department of Biblical and Theological Studies that includes both categories but offers different emphases (at the undergraduate level) or even different degrees (at the graduate level) for each. This is why in each of the main chapters of this book I illustrate the research process with one biblical studies paper (a study of the tearing of the veil in Mark's Gospel) and one theological studies paper (a study of divine accommodation in John Calvin). These two papers follow the same basic research process, but the particulars vary enough that it will be helpful for you to focus on one example or the other, depending on which one corresponds more closely to the paper you are writing.

The word *theological* may also point more broadly to all of the areas of study noted above. Fuller Theological Seminary, where I began exploring the ideas in this book, has a School of Theology that includes not only systematic and historical theology but biblical studies, philosophy and practical theology as well. This way of using the term is closer to how I use it throughout the book. As a matter of my own training and experience I focus on the traditional core disciplines of biblical studies, systematic theology and historical theology, but the basic framework of this book could be applied to other disciplines in varying degrees. Archaeology, for example, involves both an analysis component, for which this book may be useful at certain stages, and a field component, for which this book will not be useful at all.

The most important thing to keep in mind is that this book is not about "exegesis" or "hermeneutics" or "biblical interpretation." The practical goal of this book is to give you the simplest possible version of a process called theological research that is not covered in your class or curriculum. If you are working on a Bible or theology degree, you almost certainly have required courses in exegetical method, hermeneutics, Bible study methods and the like. If you've taken that course or those courses you know that the process of interpreting Scripture is anything but simple. And if you haven't taken it yet, your professor will be more than happy to recommend his or her top three (or thirty!) books on those topics. And if you're in that course right now, consider this book a supplementary resource: your professor is telling you what to do with the biblical text, and this book is going to tell you how to join those who are already doing precisely that.

Primary sources.[6] The term *primary source* can mean different things in different contexts. First, it can refer to

---

[6]See appendix C for where to find the best modern editions of your primary sources.

the single object of your research. If you are writing a paper on a specific text of Scripture, that text is your primary source. If you are writing a book review, that book is your primary source. Second, *primary source* can refer more broadly to sources that are contemporary with (written during roughly the same time period as) your subject matter. Primary sources for researching a Scripture passage can include the rest of that Scripture book (e.g., all of Romans for a paper on Romans 3), other literature by the same author (the Pauline corpus) and other literature from that time period (other first-century authors).[7]

This latter sense of *primary sources* creates a problem: there are a lot of them! A lot of people wrote a lot of literature during the first century, and even though a large percentage of that literature has not survived to the present day, enough of it has that you can hardly read all of it in a single semester (or a lifetime, for that matter). How will

---

[7]The importance of treating only contemporaneous sources as primary sources is sometimes forgotten in popular literature on the Bible. For example, there are some fun and even profound points to be made by comparing Jesus' calling and training of his disciples with the ways that Jewish rabbis called and trained their disciples. But nearly all of what we know about the rabbinic customs on this point comes from the second, third or fourth century AD, and there are concrete historical reasons (e.g., the destruction of the temple in AD 70 and its impact on Jewish religious practices) to question whether the rabbinic customs in the third century were in force during the life of Jesus. At the very least, we must admit that we do not know if those practices were in place, and so we must exercise caution in treating them as if they were.

you know which ones to read for your project? You can start by asking yourself three questions.

First, is a particular <u>primary source *relevant*</u> to the object of your research? Relevance is chiefly a function of two things:

- Continuity of subject matter (If you want to understand Barth's famous commentary on Romans, read what other German scholars were saying about Romans in the early decades of the twentieth century.)

- Specific historical relevance (If you want to understand Paul's discussion of the Jew-Gentile relationship in Romans, you'll want to be aware of Suetonius's discussion in his *Life of Claudius* regarding the expulsion of Jews from Rome a few years previous.)

The use of primary sources (plural) to understand your primary source (singular) is fraught with peril. It is easy and rhetorically exciting to take a single historical fact (X), bring it to bear on a text (Y), and claim that the meaning of the text (Z) is derived from that fact. But it is rarely the case that X + Y = Z. The expulsion of Jews from Rome in AD 49, for example, is one piece of the historical puzzle that lies behind the Jew-Gentile dynamics in the Roman church in AD 56 (when Paul probably wrote Romans). This does not mean we can take that fact and derive from it a particular interpretation of any one phrase or argument in Romans without taking many other historical and cultural and textual factors into account. It is almost never the case that one external factor will be determinative of an author's meaning at any given point. The fact that a primary source is relevant to your research question does not mean it is conclusive for the answer to that question. Treat your relevant primary sources (plural) as parts of an integrated picture of the world from which your primary source (singular) emerges, not keys to unlocking particular mysteries in the source itself.

Second, is a particular primary source *necessary* for understanding the object of your research? This is a matter of degrees, of course, and rather subjective at that. How important is Mark's transfiguration account for understanding Matthew's? It depends on your view of the redactional relationship between the two (did Matthew use Mark as a source, or vice versa?). As a starting point, the best way to determine the necessary primary texts for your research is to ask your professor. Ultimately, though, the proof is in the pudding. Can you demonstrate a deeper engagement with your primary source (singular) as a result of your engagement with your relevant primary sources (plural)? More precisely, does your thesis require your use of these sources?

Third, is it necessary for *your* research, given its scope, the nature of the course and the time constraints under which you are working? There are lots of Jewish and Greco-Roman texts written during the first century that aid our understanding of Paul's letters—they are both contemporary and relevant—but you cannot read all of them! The best way to determine whether examination of those sources is necessary is to ask your professor. In some cases, dealing with these sources will set your paper apart from the pile; in others, it will simply distract you from your central primary source (Paul's letters, in this case).

Secondary sources. To call a source *secondary* is to say that it does not coincide with the object of your research but rather points back to the object of your research. A commentary on Romans, whether written by St. Augustine in the fifth century or Karl Barth in the twentieth century, is a secondary source for a research paper on Romans. Journal articles written in the 1960s about Germany in the 1940s are secondary sources. If you are writing a book review, other book reviews written on that book can serve as secondary sources.

Secondary sources have two important functions in your research paper. First, they *guide your interaction with the primary sources*. For instance, a good commentary will take you to the text and facilitate your interaction with it, raising questions you hadn't thought to ask and bringing to the surface issues you hadn't noticed. Second, they *bring you into the conversation in which your paper is seeking a voice*. Research is like walking into a room in which several people are seated, deep in conversation—these people are your secondary sources. Your task is to sit down with them,

understand what they are talking about and add something to their discussion.

Tertiary sources. As secondary sources are written
about primary sources, tertiary sources are written about
secondary sources. In order to determine whether a particular source is secondary or tertiary, ask yourself the following question: *Is this source making an argument about
a particular issue, or is it only explaining what other sources
have argued about a particular issue?* If the former is true,
you have a secondary source; if the latter, you have a tertiary source.[8]

If you are new to your topic and don't know where to
start, tertiary sources can be extremely helpful. If you
come into the project already having a broad understanding of your area of interest, you may be able to jump
right into the primary and secondary sources. Even here,
however, it is a good idea to go back to the tertiary sources
at some point to see if you missed anything obvious. One
of the very last things I did when writing my dissertation
was to go back to the bibliographies given in certain commentaries and dictionary articles to make sure I hadn't
missed a key source.

The most helpful tertiary sources are usually dictionary

---

[8]Many secondary sources will include a summary of viewpoints or a
survey of recent scholarship on their issue. The important issue is
whether the particular section of the source you are interacting with
is secondary or tertiary.

articles, such as those in the *Dictionary of Jesus and the Gospels* or the *Anchor Bible Dictionary*.[9] Some tertiary book series also exist, such as the set of books titled *What Are They Saying About* (*the Formation of Pauline Churches, Papal Primacy, the Letter to the Hebrews, Environmental Ethics, the Parables*, etc.)? The journal *Currents in Biblical Research* can serve as a tertiary source provided that your topic is already somewhat narrow. In many cases, your textbooks for the course can serve as tertiary sources.[10] And, finally, you should think of your professor and other professors as tertiary sources. They are the ones who write the books and the articles, after all![11]

It is important to keep in mind that interaction with primary sources is the goal of your research. Unless the assignment specifically states otherwise ("summarize and

---

[9]Essays in these dictionaries may be useful secondary sources as well. You will have to use your judgment to determine which category best identifies a particular essay. See appendix C for a more complete list.

[10]Textbooks sometimes have a "resources for further study" section at the end of each chapter or unit; these are a great place to find entry-level secondary sources.

[11]One small but important point about thinking of *people* as tertiary sources: There is nothing wrong with personal conversations, Q&A sessions and email exchanges about a research topic, especially if the person with whom you are in dialogue is a scholar whose voice carries weight in your research area. I strongly encourage you to have these dialogues! But their purpose is to stimulate your thinking and point you toward the right secondary sources; they are not themselves secondary sources. Tertiary sources should rarely show up in your footnotes.

evaluate the current state of research on post–Vatican II Roman Catholic soteriology"), secondary and tertiary sources are means to the end of understanding the primary sources, not ends in themselves.

Research bibliography. Have you ever said, "I'm basically done with my paper; I just need to do the bibliography"? A bibliography is a list of sources that you put at the end of your paper in order to say, "These are the sources I *used* in researching and writing this paper." A research bibliography, however, is a list of sources that you compile from the very beginning of your project in order to say, "These are the sources I *plan to use* in researching and writing this paper." If your tertiary sources point you to a particular journal article, write down the necessary information on that article in your research bibliography. If you are in the library just before it closes and you see a reference book you will need to come back to the next day, write it down in your research bibliography. If you notice frequent references in commentaries to a particular book or essay on your topic, put it in your research bibliography.

The point of having a research bibliography is to keep track of sources so that you can come back to them later. You will not remember every journal article, book and commentary you come across in your database searches. Nor should you, every time you come across a potential source, stop what you are doing, find that source, read it cover to cover, and not come back to your search before you are finished with that source. If you notice a potential source, put it in your research bibliography. There will be time to read it later. And when your paper is written, you will simply take your research bibliography, delete the sources that turned out to be irrelevant to your paper and attach it to the back of your paper (with proper formatting, of course).

A question may have occurred to you at this point: *Where* do I record my research bibliography? Note cards? Handwritten sheets of paper? A Microsoft Word or Pages or Nota Bene document? In my head? The extremely important answer: none of the above! Let me introduce you to your new best friend: bibliography software. You can look at appendix E for a more detailed discussion, but for now I'll just say this: you should never handwrite bibliographic information. Ever. Nor—this is the really exciting part!—should you type out your bibliography in your word processor. Ever. There are bibliography software programs available that will do the work for you, as long as you learn to use them properly. My favorite happens to be Zotero, so I focus on that one in this book.

Scholarly sources. Professors will often note in their syllabi that your research must concern itself with "scholarly" sources. What does that mean? Recognizing the difference between scholarly and nonscholarly sources is not as simple as going to the library and heading to the proper floor. However, there are some basic guidelines that will enable you to make sure you are using the right kind of sources.[12]

First, scholarly sources have been *peer reviewed*. In other words, scholars other than the author have read the work and, whether or not they share its perspective, have stated that the article is worth the paper it is printed on. Online databases such as ATLA and JSTOR (see appendix D) have convenient search functions that allow you to only look for peer-reviewed journals.

Second, scholarly sources *interact with sources*. There is a difference between quoting sources and interacting with sources. To interact with a source means to enter into conversation with it, to read it, think about, evaluate it and explain the relationship between its conclusions and your own. To say it another way, scholarly means the author did *their* research, and so their comments have the potential to be helpful for *your* research. A source with no interaction with other sources, no footnotes or endnotes, and little to no bibliography is essentially saying "my opinion

---

[12]These guidelines are specifically designed for secondary and tertiary sources; primary sources are seldom scholarly in this way. Nor do they necessarily apply to many premodern sources. Thomas Aquinas did not cite sources in his *Summa Theologiae* in the same way that modern texts do, nor did his work undergo a formal peer review process such as we have today, but that does not mean he cannot serve as a secondary source on a variety of topics. Remember: above all else, a valid secondary source is one that deals closely with the primary source.

is the one that matters on this issue, so I am not concerned with what others think."[13]

A third way to know whether a source is scholarly is to check appendix C in the back of this book. The list of journals, commentaries and publishers there is by no means comprehensive, but is sufficient to set you on your way. Distinguishing scholarly from nonscholarly sources becomes easier over time, because scholarly sources refer to each other. More often than not, any source quoted or referenced in one scholarly source will itself be a scholarly source.

THEOLOGICAL RESEARCH: THE METHOD

The meat of this book is about the process of moving from topic (assignment) to thesis (argument). That process involves five steps: *finding direction, gathering*

---

[13]Keep in mind that what is true of your sources is true for your own paper! Be aware as well that there are exceptions to this point: sometimes a major scholar will write an essay that is more reflective than scholarly in appearance, and some scholarly publications have simply determined in advance that they will keep footnotes to a minimum for a variety of reasons. One helpful illustration of this is Richard Bauckham's *The Theology of the Book of Revelation* (Cambridge: Cambridge University Press, 1993), widely regarded as one of the most important books on Revelation written in many years. Bauckham's book has a total of 73 footnotes in 164 pages, which is not very many for a scholarly volume (I recently read a book on Hebrews that had 787 footnotes in 271 pages), but it is beyond dispute that Bauckham did his research and has produced a scholarly source in this case.

sources, understanding issues, entering discussion and *establishing position*. You should recognize from the outset that this process is not always linear. You will find a few sources, read them, and then go back and find a few more. You will have a thesis, but it will be faulty in some way— so you will go back and do more research. You will especially move back and forth between *gathering sources* and *understanding issues* (see chapters two and three). This will become clearer as you work your way through each step, but keep in mind that moving backwards is sometimes part of the deal, and you should not be discouraged if you are forced to do so.

You will get the most out of this book if you work your way through it as you are doing your project. Read a step, then go do it. When you think you have completed the step, come back and read it again, checking the keys to the step and comparing them with your work thus far. If you are satisfied, move on to the next step.

one

FINDING DIRECTION

EVERY RESEARCH PAPER begins with a broad topic. Your first task is to begin narrowing your topic so that you can keep your project within reasonable limits. The length of time required for this step will depend on two things: the specificity of your original assignment and your prior exposure to the topic. These same two factors will determine whether you begin with your primary sources or with your tertiary sources. If you have a specific topic or are already comfortable with your area of interest, begin with the primary sources and then go to the tertiary sources. If you have a broad topic or are completely new to the field, begin with the tertiary sources and then go to the primary sources.

KEYS TO FINDING DIRECTION

The first key to finding direction is that *you should not come into the research process having already decided what your paper is going to argue*. The entire task of theological research is to get you to the point of having something to argue. If you choose your argument in advance, you will either ignore the research that pushes against your conclusion or you will run the risk of getting to the day before your paper is due and realizing that you do not have a valid argument. This does not mean that you cannot have a specific idea that you want to consider—it simply means you cannot determine the outcome of your research in advance.

The second key is that *research takes time*. In the past, you may have been able to write lengthy papers the night before they were due and receive above-average grades on them. This simply cannot be done with a research paper. There is no such thing as good last-minute research. When you walk into a room where a conversation is taking place, it takes more than a few seconds to understand where the conversation is headed. The same is true for research.[1]

The third key is that *in the initial phase of your research, you should not touch a secondary source*. If you are researching a text of Scripture, this means no commentaries. If you are researching a historical figure, ignore later evaluations of that figure. If you are doing

---

[1] The timeline of your research will depend on several factors (the length of the term, the length of the paper, your familiarity with the topic coming in, etc.). See appendix F for a suggested timeline based on a sixteen-week course.

an in-depth book review, do not read other book reviews. This is not motivated by some mythical objectivism.[2] It is for two reasons: (1) to enable you to see the big picture in the tertiary sources before getting lost in the endless details of the secondary literature, and (2) to make sure that the focus of your research remains on the primary sources.

The fourth key to finding direction is that *this is the only stage at which you will depend heavily on tertiary sources.* This means a couple of things. On the one hand, it means that if you find yourself needing to read about basic concepts within your area of interest that are most accessible through tertiary sources, you are still on step one of the research process. On the other hand, it means that if you are past step one and are working with secondary literature, tertiary sources will not give you the kind of detail that you need for a research paper. Unless you're describing the state of the discussion on a given topic, which may be necessary in your introduction, you will rarely cite a tertiary source in a research paper. Their purpose is to *introduce* you to a topic. Get what you need from them and move on.

---

[2]In the introduction to one recent attempt to summarize the theology of the whole Bible in a single large volume, the author states that he wrote the first four drafts of the book before he looked at a single secondary source, as though avoiding other perspectives made his own more reliable.

QUESTIONS TO ASK THE TERTIARY SOURCES:

1. What are the *relevant* and *necessary* primary sources? If you know the answer to this question, you should already be reading those primary sources. But particularly when studying a historical figure, a tertiary source can help narrow your field of interest without you having to read *everything* that might or might not count as a primary source.[3]

2. Who are the key people? You cannot read everyone who has ever written on your topic, but a good tertiary source will guide you to the scholars who have made significant contributions to your area of interest.

3. What are the key works? Keep this in mind for later; if every tertiary and secondary source you read refers to a particular journal article, for example, you need to get that article.

4. What are the key issues? Remember that you are coming into a conversation that has been going on for some time. That does not mean you are never allowed to change the subject! But you need to know what the conversation is generally about before you can join it.

---

[3]You will be astounded by the volume of literature produced by many significant figures from Christian history. Choosing one of those figures and committing yourself to reading everything they wrote in order to find a research topic is not the way to go.

QUESTIONS TO ASK THE PRIMARY SOURCES[4]

1. Which portions are clearly relevant to the topic you already have in place (however broad that may be)? You'll have to read more than just these sections to capture the flow of your primary text(s), but identifying them will narrow your focus just enough to get the research process started.

2. What issues within those portions strike you as particularly interesting? This question is subject to the specificity of the assigned topic, but if your professor has left it open-ended, you might as well pursue a topic that excites you! Don't worry about what has or hasn't been said about those issues in the secondary literature—for now you need to be more concerned with finding an issue that can keep your attention for the next several weeks.

3. What are some *possible* arguments you could make? You don't need to worry about having a refined thesis here; this is merely to get you thinking about making an argument that is based on the primary sources.

---

[4]This brief section veils a host of complicated issues; precisely how we should read primary sources always has been and always will be a topic of heated debate. All I offer here are a few basic and relatively universal guidelines for listening carefully to what those sources have to say.

FINDING DIRECTION: MARK AND THE
KINGDOM OF GOD

At the end of each step, you will find descriptions of two
research papers I've written that illustrate the practical re-
alities of the step. Since students usually take some combination of biblical and theological courses, I have included one from each discipline. The first example comes
from a seminary course on the Gospels in which I was
assigned an 8–10 page research paper on the kingdom of
God in the Gospel of Mark. The second comes from a
graduate course on the doctrine of God in which the professor simply asked us to write a 15–20 page paper per-
taining to the topic of the course.

For the first paper—on the kingdom of God in the
Gospel of Mark—the primary source was obvious: the
Gospel according to Mark. So the first step in my research
was to read through Mark, looking for references to the
kingdom of God or topics that appeared to be, for Mark,
connected to the kingdom of God. In brief, I came up with
four major areas that held potential for further research:
Jesus' *teaching* about the kingdom, Jesus' *miracles* in relation to the kingdom, the *expansion* of the kingdom
through Jesus' ministry, and *opponents* of the kingdom.
And though I did not go this route, it would also have been
acceptable at this time to narrow my focus to a particular
passage (e.g., the "secret of the kingdom" in Mk 4:13-25).

Next, I spent some time reading the article titled "Kingdom of God" in the *Dictionary of Jesus and the Gospels,* paying particular attention to the section on Mark's Gospel. From this I gleaned a short list of names and secondary sources, such as William Wrede's *The Messianic Secret,* Albert Schweitzer's *The Quest of the Historical Jesus* and C. H. Dodd's *The Parables of the Kingdom.*[5] I came into this research with limited exposure to Mark's Gospel and to the concept of the kingdom of God, so it was necessary for me to read at least one tertiary source for the purpose of basic introduction to my topic, and in retrospect, reading a few more of them wouldn't have been a bad idea. You will have to decide for yourself whether or not this is necessary for each research paper.

FINDING DIRECTION: CALVIN'S DOCTRINE OF DIVINE ACCOMMODATION

It was much harder to get started with my paper on the doctrine of God. I couldn't simply pull the primary source(s) off the shelf and start reading! The more open-

---

[5]If you are familiar with this topic, you'll know that these three books are all several decades (or more) old. In a discussion as complicated and intense as the kingdom of God in the Gospels, I needed to know about these books not necessarily in order to use them as key secondary sources, but in order to understand the nature of the conversation over the past century so as to grasp more fully the more recent scholarship that became my immediate conversation partners.

ended the assignment, the more important it is to be patient. This is especially the case with a topic about which you know very little at the outset. The biggest mistake you can make is to decide too much too early. Devote the first few weeks of the course to paying careful attention to the lectures, class discussions and assigned reading, and let them be your guide in evaluating potential research topics.

Not long into the course, we began discussing John Calvin's doctrine of accommodation, which states that God adjusts himself to human capacities in order to reveal himself to us in ways that we can actually understand. I latched on to this topic for my research paper for three reasons. First, it automatically limited my primary source: the writings of John Calvin.[6] Second, I knew that by using words like "accommodation" and "John Calvin" in my database searches, I could hone in on the right secondary sources rather quickly. Third, I thought I could connect this project to a previous writing project on divine theophanies in the Old Testament. Since the doctrine of accommodation is concerned with how God reveals himself, biblical narratives wherein God actually does that in some tangible way offered a way for me to overlap one issue about which I knew very little with another issue about which I knew a fair bit more.

---

[6]John Calvin wrote quite a lot, so this might not seem very helpful. But given my starting point—"the doctrine of God"—it was a step in the right direction!

My first task was to narrow the scope of my search. Rather than writing a single treatise on the doctrine of accommodation, Calvin discussed this doctrine in hundreds of places throughout his *Institutes* and biblical commentaries. So I began by checking the subject index of the *Institutes*, and since I was interested in relating the doctrine of accommodation to Old Testament theophanies, I read his commentaries on those texts. I also found some very brief descriptions of accommodation in introductory volumes to Calvin, where I learned that an essay written in 1977 by Ford L. Battles titled "God Was Accommodating Himself to Human Capacity" was probably the most important essay on my topic.[7]

Keys to Finding Direction

1. Do not come into the research process having already decided what your paper is going to argue.
2. Research takes time.
3. In the initial phase of your research, you should not touch a secondary source.
4. This is the only stage at which you will depend heavily on tertiary sources.

---

[7]Ford L. Battles, "God Was Accommodating Himself to Human Capacity," *Interpretation* 31 (1977): 19-38.

two

GATHERING SOURCES

AT THIS POINT, YOU SHOULD HAVE four things: (1) broad familiarity with your primary source, (2) some exposure to the issues associated with your general topic, (3) more than one idea for the direction of your paper, and (4) the beginnings of a research bibliography based on the tertiary sources. Your next task is to begin gathering and working through the secondary sources to which the tertiary sources have pointed you. Start with these particular sources, and use them as a springboard into the rest of the secondary literature. Many of the texts you need are in your school library, either in the stacks or in the reference section; if you need a book that your library doesn't have, talk to your librarian about interlibrary loan options if you are not already familiar with those systems at your institution. If you need a journal article, start by looking on ATLA (see appendix D). If ATLA offers neither a PDF nor a link to one, try the printed journal stacks at your library. If that doesn't work, try interlibrary loan.[1]

KEYS TO GATHERING SOURCES

The first key to gathering secondary sources is that *you should not spend too much time on any one source*. This is not yet the time to be reading deeply. When you obtain a potential source, skim it quickly. Don't worry about whether you agree with its conclusions or whether it has any particular arguments that support or oppose the direction of your paper. If your source is a library book, don't check it out immediately. Take it off the shelf, give it a quick read, and then decide whether it is worth carrying home. If it's a reference book that you can't check out, don't photocopy it yet. Make sure it has at least some relevance to your project before you spend the money. If it's an article from ATLA available in PDF form, don't print it yet. Download it to your computer and skim through it before you waste paper on something you don't need.

The second thing to remember is that *there is a fine line between redirecting and getting distracted*. You will find

---

[1]Don't let the accessibility of a book or article determine whether or not you "need" it for your research: full-text versions of journal articles appear on ATLA because the journal in which they appear subscribes to that service, not because they are more important. There are limits to this—if only two libraries in the world have a particular source, or if it only exists on microfiche, there's a good chance you can get by without it.

yourself being pulled in different directions by the issues being emphasized in the sources, and you need to remember that a research paper is not an opportunity to read random articles on all the topics that interest you. But at any point along the way, your research may lead you in a direction you were not previously aware of, and that is permissible. Simply keep in mind three things: that your goal is to *narrow* your topic, not *broaden* it, that this particular assignment has a deadline, and that you have other assignments besides this one that require your attention.

The third key is that *not every important source will be well written*. Some sources will make you wonder if you and the author are using the same language. Some sources will make you feel that you simply are not smart enough for serious research because you don't understand what they are talking about. It may be that you need to look up unfamiliar terms in a dictionary, or that you have not spent enough time in the tertiary sources to move comfortably through the secondary literature. Or it simply may be that scholar X is not a good writer. The point is that you should not be intimidated or discouraged by the fact that even skimming secondary sources can be slow going.

The fourth and final key is to *remember that research is first and foremost about primary sources*. As you continue to narrow your topic through searching for secondary sources, always come back to your primary source(s) to make sure that you are pursuing a legitimate issue.

QUESTIONS TO ASK THE SECONDARY SOURCES

1. Does this source handle your primary source(s)? If a book or article makes little or no reference to your primary source, go no further. You don't have time for it.

2. Is it a scholarly source? (See *scholarly sources* under "Defining Key Terms" in the introduction.) If not, go no further. You don't have time for it.

3. Does it deal with one or more of the issues you have identified from the primary source(s) as being possible topics for your paper? Or does it bring out an issue that you missed in the primary source(s) that could also serve as a possible topic?

4. Does it point you toward more secondary sources that may be useful for your project? If so, put those other sources in your research bibliography, and when you are ready, go through the same process with those sources. Remember that your source can only interact with other sources that are *older* than it—be aware of the chronological development of the conversation on your topic.

GATHERING SOURCES: MARK AND THE KINGDOM OF GOD

I began gathering sources by referring to my research bibliography (from the tertiary sources) and by doing an

ATLA search for "Mark" and "kingdom of God." I found several sources interested in Jesus' teaching of the kingdom of God in Mark, particularly concerning the so-called Messianic Secret and Jesus' parables. I also found plenty of literature on the role of demonic forces in opposition to Jesus' ministry. A third area of interest concerned the conflict in Mark's Gospel between the kingdom of God and the current temple establishment (which also falls within the broad category of opposition to Jesus and the kingdom of God). I chose to pursue this third option.

Having narrowed my topic to this degree, I went back to the Gospel of Mark to do my own research on the issue of Jesus and his opposition from the temple authorities. The questions to ask at this point are basically the same as those brought to the primary source in step one: finding direction. Is "Jesus vs. the temple authorities" a valid research topic under the rubric of "The kingdom of God in Mark's Gospel"? What does Mark himself have to say about the issue? Once you have asked these questions and spent more time in your primary source(s), you may return to the secondary literature and continue building your research bibliography.

GATHERING SOURCES: CALVIN'S DOCTRINE OF ACCOMMODATION

I knew from my previous research that Ford L. Battles's essay on Calvin's doctrine of accommodation would be critical to my research, so I read that essay first. In it I found Calvin's most basic use of the doctrine, where in response to those who thought Scripture ascribed to God a literal physical body he argued that "such forms of speaking [God's hands, ears, etc.] do not so much express clearly what God is like as accommodate the knowledge of him to our slight capacity" (*Institutes* 1.13.1).

I noticed, however, that while Battles had a lot to say about Calvin's *Institutes*, he made almost no reference to Calvin's commentaries. Since I had already found lots of discussion of accommodation in those commentaries, I wondered if some emphasis on Calvin's doctrine of accommodation in a particular Scripture passage might be worth pursuing. And since Battles's essay was over thirty years old, I needed to find some more recent sources.

In subsequent reading I made two important discoveries. First, scholars noted that Calvin had a lot to say about God accommodating himself during the Sinai theophanies (Ex 19–34). Second, I found a lot of criticism of Calvin's doctrine of accommodation. These criticisms usually took on either a philosophical (If the God we see isn't like the God who exists, has God really revealed himself?) or exegetical (Does Scripture present a God who reveals something other than who he truly is?) flavor. Since my background was stronger on the exegetical side, I decided to see whether Calvin's doctrine of accommodation resulted in a fair reading of the Sinai theophanies.

In other words, my research question had become, "Does Calvin's doctrine of accommodation adequately describe God's self-revelation at Mount Sinai as that event is described in Exodus 19–34?" At this point, I needed to return to my primary sources: Exodus 19–34 and Calvin's commentaries on those texts.

EXCURSUS ONE
Common Research Mistakes with Sources

Using nonscholarly sources such as devotional commentaries, op-ed articles and blogs. These sources can be useful for stimulating your own thinking about a text or issue—I'm not saying you shouldn't read them! But a research paper is a foray into a *scholarly* conversation, and so your conversation partners need to be *scholarly* sources. Concretely, this means you should not cite them in your paper or include them in your bibliography, unless your specific project calls for these kinds of sources.

Citing the Internet. It is rarely a good idea to cite an online source, unless your research topic specifically demands it. Using an article from an online database such as ATLA is different because you are citing a specific printed source that happens to exist on a website, not the website itself. You can also use full-text databases such as books.google.com or amazon.com for the same reason: these sites contain the printed source in digital form and are not sources in and of themselves (as a blog post that claims to quote your source would be). You should avoid on-line sources for these reasons: (1) online sources are almost never peer reviewed, (2) online sources often misquote their sources, if they cite sources at all,[a] (3) Internet links change frequently, so it can be difficult for your professor or grader to check the accuracy of your interaction with online sources, and (4) the proper formatting of internet source references in your footnotes and bibliography is far more difficult and complicated than that of printed sources, so you are only making more work for yourself. As in the first point, I strongly recommend only citing online sources if your project specifically calls for it.

Using only sources that you agree with. This is begging your professor to believe that either (1) you did very little research and only quoted those you had already read coming into the project, or (2) your thesis is weak and you intentionally ignored the evidence pointing away from it. Presenting and interacting with the evidence *against* your thesis is a critical part of a research paper.

Using only one type of source.[b] Commentaries have a particular role in the academic conversation, as do journal articles, dissertations, essays, monographs and dictionary articles. Using only one or two of these will restrict the scope of your research, while using all of them will broaden your perspective and strengthen your research. On any given issue or portion of your paper you may need to interact more with one type of source than another, but on the whole you should include some dialogue with all of them.

Considering only one subdiscipline. Some of your sources will emphasize literary issues, some will focus on historical aspects of the topic, some will highlight geographical insights and others will be interested in the theological end of things. Your research needs to include all relevant subdisciplines. You may present a thesis that specifically deals with only one of these ("the geographical issues involved with the conquest of Jericho have impact X on the interpretation of that narrative . . ."). Even in this case, one subdiscipline cannot be isolated from the others. Historical and literary issues will influence the way the geography should be viewed and vice versa.

---

[a]For an illustration of potential problems with online sources, check out this extremely in-depth analysis by Peter M. Head, Sir Kirby Laing Senior Fellow in New Testament at Tyndale House, Cambridge, of a Wikipedia article dealing with biblical textual criticism: evangelicaltextualcriticism.blogspot.com/2015/02/wikipedia-is-still-bad-notes-on-codex.html.

[b]Commentaries are a particularly attractive danger in this regard for research on a particular text of Scripture because they are so easy to find and so easy to use. But commentaries are often short-and-sweet compendiums of the research found in journal articles and essays and monographs—unless you are dealing with a particularly controversial issue—and in most cases will not offer the depth of analysis you need. There are some exceptionally thorough commentaries, of course, but even then you need to broaden the scope of your inquiry.

Keys to Gathering Sources

1. Do not spend too much time on any one source.
2. There is a fine line between redirecting and getting distracted.
3. Not every important source will be well written.
4. Research is first and foremost about primary sources.

three

UNDERSTANDING ISSUES

MOST OF WHAT YOU HAVE DONE up to this point has been background work: learning the language, gaining tools and familiarity with those tools, and finding your way around the shop, so to speak. Now it's time to begin your project. Your goal in this next phase is to learn as much as you can from your sources about the specific issues involved with your topic. What arguments are being made? What are the reasons for and against those arguments? And, as before, remember that your primary source is the final arbiter in nearly every debate.

KEYS TO UNDERSTANDING ISSUES

Most of your time in this phase will be spent reading. The first key to getting what you need out of your reading in the least amount of time is to *read with your pen (or pencil)*. If you have an article downloaded from ATLA, print it out. If you're reading a book that you own, be prepared to make notes in it. If you have a book or journal that you do not

own, photocopy the relevant pages. Never mark a source
that does not belong to you!

I prefer to write on printed sources instead of taking
notes on a separate piece of paper or digitally (either in
a word processor or in note-taking software such as
Endnote). The problem with recording notes separately
is that doing so requires a shift in focus from one
medium (the source) to another (your computer/paper),
breaking your concentration and preventing you from
reading well.[1] It may be useful to skim back through
your printed sources (and the notes you have made on
them) in order to type out more comprehensive notes
just prior to beginning the writing process, but don't try
to do that as you go.

You need to have a system for your reading. For instance, I put a star next to sections that I find particularly
helpful. I write "agree?" in the margins next to statements
I want to think about more deeply or that I think are

---

[1]Keep in mind that doing research and reading textbooks are two
different things. When you read a textbook, you may need to take
notes separately as you go in order to cement in your memory certain details: dates, names, places, sequences, definitions, etc. In research you don't care about memorizing all the details; you care
about comprehending an argument and grasping the points at which
that argument connects (positively or negatively) with yours. Unlike
an exam, where you have to remember all of the relevant data, writing a research paper involves constant reference back to your research. If you need to include a piece of data in your paper, look it
up at the appropriate time instead of trying to memorize it.

questionable. If I come across an argument in one article that is either similar to or precisely in disagreement with an argument in another article, I write "see p. 259 in Hays" or something similar in the margin. However you choose to do this, have a consistent method so that when you return to a source and see a particular notation, you know what you meant when you wrote it.

A brief excursus on underlining and highlighting: Some of us underline or highlight as a function of reading itself— to mark a sentence in one of these ways is simply to say "I read that and understood it." This is a *bad* idea! When you're done, you'll have a source that is almost entirely underlined or highlighted, and all you will have accomplished is to add clutter to the page and make it even harder to go back later and recall the important parts.[2] If you underline or highlight at all, do so consistently for one specific reason that will make it easier, not harder, to return to the source later in the research process. You might, for example, underline or highlight the basic components of the argument in that source. Look for the words "my thesis is that . . ." or "this essay will argue that . . ." in the first few paragraphs of the source. Highlight or underline that sentence and write "THESIS" in the margin. Then, each time a successive piece of that argument appears, highlight or

---

[2]If the source in question happens to be a book you own, this also cuts significantly into its resale value!

underline the precise words that return to the thesis. This will enable you to quickly recall the basic argument of any given source and find particular elements of that argument within the body.

The second key to working through your sources is that *you must allow yourself large time segments* for doing so. You cannot read a paragraph, go to class, come back and read another paragraph, get dinner, then come back for a third paragraph, and expect to make progress in your research. Your ability to grasp what a source is saying about your topic is dependent on your ability to read through and think through the entire source, or at least an entire section of the source, without interruption. If you're reading an article, perhaps fifteen or twenty pages long, force yourself to read the whole article without stopping. If you're reading a book, focus on getting through an entire chapter at a time.[3] This can be difficult (I speak as one who tried to do research while taking care of an infant), but it is a critical part of entering into the conversation and understanding the issues being discussed there.

Allowing yourself large time segments for reading involves more than working through a source in one sitting—it involves working through that source without being

---

[3]Only rarely will you need to read a book in its entirety. If the whole book is written on your exact topic, your topic is most likely too broad. More often you will only need a chapter or two from a book on a broader topic.

distracted by the world around you, especially the electronic world. You can't do research and watch the game simultaneously; you can only move back and forth between the two at a rapid pace. Checking Facebook interrupts your research no less than taking a coffee break. Reading well means reading without engaging other mediums, especially for those of us who are addicted to the grid, electronic mediums.

The third key to remember is that *you are not reading sources for their own sake, but rather for the sake of your paper.* If a book has two chapters that concern your topic, read those two chapters and spend as little time as possible on the rest of the book. If the larger topic of the book (or another chapter in that book) interests you, write it down and come back to it later. You have a limited amount of time in which to complete your paper, and you will not want to waste it on sources that are interesting but do not relate to your topic. You can always make a note to come back to that fascinating-but-irrelevant-to-your-thesis point another time. Remember that secondary sources are a means to an end, not ends in and of themselves.

The fourth key to understanding the issues is that *the specificity of your sources will determine the specificity of your topic.* Perhaps you have been assigned a paper in your Hebrews course and want to write on the use of the Old Testament in Hebrews. You will quickly find that no single source covers this territory comprehensively (even if you find journal articles bearing the title "The Use of the Old Testament in Hebrews"). Instead, scholars will focus on a particular Old Testament text in Hebrews (e.g., Ps 110), a particular issue within the topic of the Old Testament in Hebrews (e.g., the version of the Greek Old Testament used by the author of Hebrews), or, more frequently, a single Old Testament text in a single portion of Hebrews (e.g., Ps 95 in Heb 3–4) or the combination of Old Testament texts in a single portion of Hebrews (e.g., the mishmash of Psalms in Heb 1). The existence of these secondary sources should tell you that your paper cannot offer a comprehensive discussion of the topic of the Old Testament in Hebrews.

The fifth key is to realize that *along the research journey, you will constantly cycle back and forth between steps two (gathering sources) and three (understanding issues)*. You may read four or five sources, three of which mention a particular article that you have not yet gotten your hands on. At that point you should repeat step two: go to the library, retrieve the source, ask the relevant questions and move on from there.

QUESTIONS TO ASK SECONDARY SOURCES:

1. Where is the discussion coming from? That is, what are some of the major positions that have been held and major shifts that have taken place over the course of the discussion?

2. Where is the discussion going *today*? You need to be relatively up to date on the interaction between your sources. You aren't writing a dissertation, where if a key author is going to publish something next month you should already know about it. But if a major shift in the discussion has taken place in the last few years or decades, your research is not complete without an awareness of that shift. For example, if you're researching Paul's view of the law and don't make note of the New Perspective on Paul, your research will be destined for failure.

3. What sorts of arguments are being made? What are some of the strengths and weaknesses of those arguments? Who stands on which side of the divide? Once you've done a fair bit of reading, you might make a list of key issues and under each one map out the options, the arguments for each option and the scholars who choose each of those options. Make sure that scholars are placed in various categories by their own admission—don't assume that because scholar X says scholar Y holds such-and-such a view it's necessarily the case. Read scholar Y for yourself to make sure you get their perspective on their own terms. If you have holes in your map (for example, many scholars note view A in order to refute it but no one you've read actually holds the view), you've got some more reading to do.

4. What might be a possible thesis, and what are the arguments for and against it? What evidence from the *primary source* is relevant for this thesis? Remember again that the Goal is not (especially at this point) to create a brand-new avenue for the conversation; it's okay if your thesis is already part of the discussion and scholars have proposed arguments for and against it.

UNDERSTANDING THE ISSUES: MARK AND THE KINGDOM OF GOD

After reading a number of secondary sources (articles, books, dissertation chapters, etc.), I determined that the discussion surrounding Jesus vs. the temple authorities in Mark's Gospel emphasized three specific events in the latter part of Mark: Jesus' prophecy of the destruction of the temple, the cursing of the fig tree and the cleansing/cursing of the temple, and the tearing of the veil at Jesus' crucifixion. I chose the last option, and so began considering different arguments I could make concerning that event. My thesis needed to look something like this: *The tearing of the veil means _____ in Mark's Gospel in the context of the conflict between Jesus and the temple authorities.* Having come to this point, I was able to search more specifically in the library and on ATLA, looking for articles and books dealing with the tearing of the veil in the Gospel of Mark.

UNDERSTANDING ISSUES: CALVIN'S DOCTRINE OF ACCOMMODATION

Once I had established my question regarding Calvin's reading of the Sinai theophanies, I needed to go back and do quite a bit more research. An interdisciplinary paper such as this one can be especially difficult because you have two streams of thought that rarely connect. That is, I needed to read essays on Calvin's doctrine of accommodation that would rarely reference Exodus 19–34, and I needed to read commentaries and articles and books on Exodus 19–34 that would not cite Calvin. I do not recommend this route *unless you have done substantial work in one of the two areas prior to beginning the paper.* I had already read quite a lot on Exodus 19–34 before engaging Calvin, so I was able to put the two together without too much difficulty. But I still needed to ask the exegetical question "How did God reveal himself at Sinai?" alongside the theological question "Is Calvin's doctrine of accommodation compatible with that revelation?"

EXCURSUS TWO
Common Research Mistakes in Interaction

The mistakes discussed in this excursus may look like *writing* mistakes rather than *research* mistakes. They are indeed mistakes that will show up in your writing, but they will because of shortcomings in your research. You need to be aware of them now so you can avoid them later.

Too much quoting. This is *your* paper, not a collection of quotes from others. If you can say it in your own words, do so (you still need a footnote or in-text citation to bring attention to your source). If you can't say it in your own words, study it until you can. Never quote a secondary source when you can paraphrase. You should only quote when you value *how* a scholar says something; if only the content itself is valuable, paraphrase.

Excessive quoting will cause trouble in two ways. First, it will lead you to believe that something is true simply because a certain prominent scholar says it is true. The value of a secondary source is in its interaction with the primary source, not in the pedigree of its author. Second, it will lead your professor to believe that you did not actually *think* about the issues at hand. You simply collected some opinions and put them into paragraph form. That is not the impression you want to leave!

Depending too much on tertiary and secondary sources. If this sounds familiar, you've been paying attention! Research is about the *primary sources*. Remember that your sources are no less susceptible to this than you are. I recently spoke with a friend working on her dissertation who wrote a chapter depending on the work of an older volume that had, as some volumes will, come into a kind of urban legend status—everyone cited it, but no one actually read it. When she went back to this older volume, she discovered that more recent scholarship supposedly depending on this volume clearly had not read it.

Misunderstanding sources. You do *not* want to receive your paper back from the professor with a note that says "I don't think you understood this source." This is especially true when you are referencing something the professor wrote!

Keys to Understanding Issues

1. Read with your pen (or pencil).
2. Allow yourself large time segments.
3. Read sources not for their own sake, but rather for the sake of your paper.
4. The specificity of your sources will determine the specificity of your topic.
5. Don't be afraid to cycle back and forth between gathering sources and understanding issues.

four

ENTERING DISCUSSION

At some point in every conversation it becomes your turn to speak. Up to this point, you've been doing a lot of listening—making sure that you understand the tone, the topic and the direction of the conversation. Now it's your turn to become a fully participating member of the conversation. It is time to talk!

KEYS TO ENTERING THE DISCUSSION

Polite conversation in any setting has certain acceptable norms. One does not enter an already-ongoing conversation and immediately change the subject. One does not repeat verbatim what has already been said, nor does one discount prior statements without giving a reason for doing so. What one says on entering that conversation must be relevant and helpful to that conversation, or one's place at the table will be called into question.

The same is true for your research paper. In short, and this is the first key to this phase of research, you need to *have something to contribute to the discussion.* This can take many forms. You may build on one specific argument that has been made. You may offer a brief summary of where the discussion is and suggest what direction it should take in the future. You may state why you agree with one position and disagree with another. You may offer a new perspective that continues the conversation but takes it in a slightly different direction.

The second key is that you must *recognize the appropriate time to enter the discussion.* How do you know when it is time to speak? Or to put it another way, how do you know when you have done enough research? I can think of four specific things to look for. First, you will know you've done enough research when your sources are conversing with each other. When your sources are interacting with each other, whether agreeing or disagreeing, you are headed in the right direction—you've come full circle in the conversation, so to speak. If you're not sure about this, take any given secondary source you've deemed important for your research and check the footnotes. Have you read the sources that this particular source deems *its* important conversation partners? Second, you've done enough research when *you* can converse with your sources. Can you read a source and notice where they've missed a point made by another source? Third, and perhaps most importantly, you've done enough research when you can picture yourself seated at a table with the four or five most significant scholars in your area of study and know that you can understand and contribute to the discussion. When you come to this point, you're ready to put your research to use. Fourth, at some point you need to be done researching because you have a deadline. There will always be more sources to read, more searches to run, more studying to do, but no matter how thorough your research, you still need time to write your paper. I recommend that you stop looking for new sources at least a week prior to your final deadline.

The third key to entering the discussion is that you must be able to *articulate how your thesis fits into the discussion*. I have already stated that you must understand the discussion and that your thesis must fit that discussion. Your reader, who may be less familiar with the discussion than you are, will not necessarily recognize *how* your thesis fits into the discussion. So as you begin to transition from reading to writing, you should keep these four questions in mind: (1) What is the specific issue? (2) What is the current conversation about that issue? (3) What is my argument concerning the specific issue? and (4) How does my argument fit into the current conversation? If you can answer these four questions comfortably, you should be ready to enter the discussion. And just so it's clear: *your paper should include your answers to these questions*.

QUESTIONS TO ASK SECONDARY SOURCES:

1. What arguments are scholars making *for* and *against*
   my thesis? If you cannot answer the latter question,
   especially, either your thesis is too easy or you have not
   done enough research.

2. Does my thesis hold up against the counterarguments?
   You should include in your paper the reasons why
   some scholars do not or would not agree with your
   conclusion, as well as your responses to those objec-
   tions. If you can't respond to them, you probably need
   to make an adjustment to your thesis.[1]

QUESTIONS TO ASK PRIMARY SOURCES:

1. What evidence has been lost in the shuffle? Are there
   any issues in the primary source that no one seems to
   be talking about? Keep in mind that if you have a long
   list of these, it may be that you haven't done enough
   research. A lot of people have been looking at your
   primary source for a long time, so there's a good chance
   someone has noticed just about everything in it.

2. Does my argument match what the primary source has
   to say? This is the obvious question from beginning to

---

[1]Be comforted by the fact that "make an adjustment" is not the same
as "throw the whole thing away and start over." A leaky roof does
not necessarily require demolition of the entire house.

end of your project. I repeat it here because at this stage it's easy to get excited about a particular argument about a particular piece of the primary source and forget that your argument can't only work with *part* of the primary source—it has to work with the whole thing.

ENTERING THE DISCUSSION: MARK AND THE KINGDOM OF GOD

In my research on the tearing of the veil in Mark 15, I came across one scholar who had cataloged approximately thirty-five different interpretations of that event! Rather than examine all thirty-five and choose one, or suggest number thirty-*six*, I chose to suggest a standard for evaluating those thirty-five interpretations based on other texts in Mark that influenced the way I believed the tearing of the veil should be understood. My sources suggested two specific texts: the baptism of Jesus in Mark 1 for its many parallels with the crucifixion narrative, and the conflict between Jesus and the temple authorities in Mark 12–13 (with the tearing of the temple veil as the climax of that conflict).

After interacting for a while with these two texts and their relationship to the tearing of the veil through the secondary sources, I returned to the primary source: Mark 15. I found a strong basis for using both of the texts mentioned above, but I also found a third that had not been mentioned in my secondary sources: the brackets around the tearing of the veil in Mark 15:38 formed by the note that

Jesus "breathed his last" in Mark 15:37 and 15:39. Therefore, I argued in my thesis that there are *three* textual relationships one must take into account when interpreting the tearing of the veil in Mark's Gospel: the baptism of Jesus, the conflict between Jesus and the temple authorities and the event of Jesus "breathing his last" at the cross. That is, our understanding of the tearing of the veil in Mark needs to be informed by these three texts in Mark to one degree or another.

You may notice that my final thesis is not obviously connected to the original topic (the kingdom of God in Mark). If your research and your interests take you outside the original parameters of the assignment, make sure you communicate with the professor in advance. Professors are often willing to hear proposals for papers that do not strictly follow the original assignment, provided that you (1) demonstrate you have already done your homework on the topic and can demonstrate how your paper answers a meaningful question and (2) you check with them *ahead of time* to make sure that they approve. It's not easier to ask forgiveness than permission in this case!

ENTERING THE DISCUSSION: CALVIN'S DOCTRINE OF ACCOMMODATION

The conversation into which you are entering via your research paper is far more complex than you realized at the outset—and if you haven't figured that out, you haven't done enough research! Good research papers acknowledge that complexity but don't try to tie up every loose end. My paper on Calvin and the Sinai theophanies had to show my professor that I was aware of some of the elements of the conversation to which I was not going to devote a great deal of attention, such as philosophical problems with divine accommodation or source-critical issues in Exodus 19–34. In such cases you will sometimes need to say "here's an issue I will not address and here's *why* I won't address it, but it is important for the broader topic, and here are some of the key secondary sources on it." But don't try to do more than that, or your paper will quickly become a tertiary source: a list of issues with lots of footnotes to the real conversation. Of course, your professor may also indicate in their evaluation that down one of those potential rabbit trails were some rather important insights that you missed, but good research (meaning you've actually *looked* at those key secondary sources rather than merely including them in a long footnote) should ward off that flaming arrow.

Exodus 19–34 recounts three theophanies: to all Israel in Exodus 19–20, to Moses and Aaron and the elders of Israel in Exodus 24 and to Moses alone in Exodus 34. So my first task was to understand what Calvin said about accommodation in those particular texts. Second, I needed to engage those texts for myself (in conversation with biblical exegetes) and articulate what I thought they said about God revealing himself. Finally, I needed to put those two tasks together in order to say whether or not Calvin's doctrine of accommodation adequately explained God's self-revelation in those three cases.

Still, my topic was too broad—God's self-revelation at Sinai is simply too complex! So I zoomed in one more time, to God's *presence* at Sinai. So I left aside whether or not God's *commands* were accommodated (which was a major topic of discussion in my secondary sources) and focused on what it might mean for God to be "on" the mountain (in Ex 19), for the elders to "see" God (in Ex 24) and for God to go "with" his people (in Ex 33–34). For Calvin, the fact that God is all-present at all times meant statements in Scripture that God was or was not in a particular place at a particular time must be accommodated in some sense.

The goal of my paper was to do something truly integrative: I not only wanted to ask whether Calvin's doctrine of accommodation stood up to exegetical scrutiny, but also what that doctrine might add to our understanding of the Sinai texts today. I quickly found that my secondary sources on Exodus (mostly modern scholars) weren't asking that question! So my essay emphasized ways that Calvin's reading of the Sinai theophanies added something to more recent interpretations of those passages. At the same time, I thought Calvin had missed some things and that his doctrine needed a little bit of refining in order to make sense of God's presence at Sinai.

When all was said and done, my thesis looked like this: "This essay contends that a dialogue between Calvin's doctrine of accommodation and the Sinai narratives will be profitable for our understanding of both, and that Calvin's doctrine is a valuable (though not infallible) tool for those wishing to speak well of God on the basis of Scripture." The final phrase was an almost-word-for-word reiteration of the main objective of the course given by the professor at the beginning of the term. When the paper is specifically required to correspond to the course objectives, as this one was, it never hurts to make it very clear to the professor that your paper does this!

Keys to Entering the Discussion

1. Do you have something to contribute to the discussion?
2. Can you recognize the appropriate time to enter the discussion?
3. Can you articulate how your thesis fits into the discussion?

five

ESTABLISHING POSITION

THE GOAL OF THIS BOOK has been to guide you along each step of your journey from *topic* (e.g., the kingdom of God in Mark) to *thesis* (e.g., there are three texts in Mark that must be taken into account by any suggested interpretation of the tearing of the veil in Mark 15:38). The final step, establishing position, is a simple one (I don't mean *easy*): write your paper! But given that this is a *research* paper, here are a couple of final keys to keep in mind.

KEYS TO ESTABLISHING POSITION

First, *your thesis is the heart and soul of your paper*. Every single word, phrase and paragraph in your paper should contribute to your thesis. If something in your paper doesn't contribute to your thesis, cut it out. Be ruthless![1]

---

[1] If you're concerned about being able to meet the minimum length requirement for your paper, you need to do more research. A well-researched paper will always struggle to stay under the maximum rather than over the minimum.

Several years ago, my boss sent me out to do some tree trimming. His basic guideline: talk to the tree. Tell it which direction you want it to grow and which direction you don't. If a branch is going the wrong direction, cut it off. Big or small, healthy or sick, pretty or hideous, if it's not going where you want it to go, get rid of it. Think of your paper as a tree, and your thesis as your chosen direction. If a paragraph or illustration or argument or word doesn't take your paper where you want it to go (as defined by your thesis), get rid of it. Your paper must offer a position. You are arguing, not merely informing.

Second, *don't start writing your paper too soon.* You may want to take notes, construct individual arguments or draw diagrams and charts. Remember, though, that if you write your paper before you have a thesis, you'll have to rewrite it. And if you write your thesis before you do your research, you won't be able to support it. The best way for you to end up with a paper that revolves around a well-supported thesis is to (1) let your research mold your thesis and (2) let your thesis mold your paper.

Third, y*our research paper should enter into an already-existing conversation about your chosen topic.* Remember that a research paper is not you thinking in a vacuum. Thus, your paper needs demonstrate three things: that you are *aware of* the conversation, that you *understand* the conversation and that you can *participate in* that conversation.

Fourth, don't be afraid to ask for help! Some professors

will give you a chance to hand in your paper early for feedback to help you prepare the final draft. The teaching assistant for your class may be available to help you find sources, construct arguments or deal with other issues. Your librarian will also be able to assist you in locating sources and using online databases. If you are new to writing academic papers and feel overwhelmed by the task in front of you, your school may have a writing center with editors available to look at your paper or sit down with you and talk through it.

Keys to Establishing Position

1. Your thesis is the heart and soul of your paper.
2. Don't start writing your paper too soon.
3. Research is entering into an already-existing conversation about your chosen topic.

CONCLUSION

FIND DIRECTION. Gather sources. Understand issues. Enter discussion. Establish position. There is something deeply satisfying about moving from chaos to order, from confusion to clarity, from ignorance to understanding. Just as we enjoy the transition from a pile of boards and screws to a fully functional desk, we can enjoy the transition from the vagueness of a *topic* to the concreteness of a *thesis*. My hope is that this book not only enables you to do theological research but also to enjoy it. I do not promise that it will be easy, but I do believe that it can be fun! So if you're skimming through this book prior to beginning your research project, now is the time to go back to step one and start gathering those primary sources.[1] If you're now at the end of your project, may you come to this point having learned some new information but also having gained confidence in a thesis that is reflected clearly in your paper and in your life.

---

[1]See appendix C to find the right editions of your primary sources.

TEN THINGS YOU SHOULD *NEVER* DO IN A THEOLOGICAL RESEARCH PAPER

I'VE ALREADY IDENTIFIED a number of common mistakes in research (see the excurses on pp. 61 and 73). Here I list the kinds of errors that are most likely to make your professors pull their hair out—what will really drive them nuts!

1. Suggest that your research paper has broken new ground. It hasn't. I promise.

2. Use terms that are the object of significant debate in your field in ways that suggest you don't know they are the object of significant debate in your field. In my dissertation proposal (a short description submitted to the PhD committee in the first year of doctoral studies), I made the mistake of using the word *canonical* to describe my chosen method for the dissertation. Did I acknowledge the recent debates over the

nature and pros and cons of canonical readings of Scripture? No. Did I get raked over the coals in my proposal defense by two scholars who had made significant contributions to those debates? Yes, and I deserved every moment of it.

3. Make personal attacks on scholars you disagree with. Never, *ever* make a personal attack in your research paper. It's rude, it's unnecessary and it begs your reader—who happens to be grading your work!— to assume that you couldn't come up with a real rebuttal to the argument, so you resorted to cheap shots. An example I see frequently in evangelical contexts: accusations about a scholar's doctrine of Scripture. It is simply not the case that because scholar X believes in theistic evolution, he or she has a "low doctrine of Scripture." Nor is it the case that because scholars Y and Z reject a particular version of the documentary hypothesis, they are fundamentalist ignoramuses who need to get their heads out of the sand. These sorts of claims have no place at all in a theological research paper (nor in late-night dorm-room conversations, for that matter).

4. Discuss how you "feel" about certain issues or viewpoints. It's not that your professor doesn't care about your feelings. It's that they are irrelevant to determining the strengths and weaknesses of your research.

5. Commit logical fallacies. You should have a list of these (with explanations) on your desk at all times. Every time you make an argument, check the list to make sure none of them apply. Better yet, take an introductory course on logic in the philosophy department at your institution.

6. Misrepresent scholarly viewpoints or arguments. Nothing will drive your professors more crazy than communicating to them that you didn't read your sources carefully.

7. Adjectivize the scholars you disagree with. Wright may be "compelling" while Bultmann is "liberal"; Webster's account may be "robust" while Frame's is "reductionistic." The problem with these words is twofold. First, they're not arguments in and of themselves. They're comparisons—they don't say anything other than where a scholar stands vis-à-vis *your* position, and unless it is taken for granted that *your* position is the right one, such descriptions are pointless and distract from the presence or absence of the real argument in your paper. Second, they make a value judgment that has not been substantiated. Is "liberal" bad? Is "robust" good? You must always define your technical terms, but these are terms that you don't have time to define, so you'll save yourself a lot of trouble if you don't use them in the first place.

8. Forget to identify your thesis. Your paper has one
   and only one central point. Make it abundantly clear
   to your reader what that point is. Do so early, and do
   so often.

9. Ignore the citation style guide required by your professor. Early in your theological research career, formatting footnotes and bibliographies will feel like ar-
   bitrary busywork, even with bibliography software to
   facilitate the process. Why bother with all that? In
   short: you need to know your audience. A research
   paper is a communicative act directed toward those
   who have spent years staring at scholarly literature to
   the point that a misplaced punctuation mark in a citation sticks out like a sore thumb and a misspelled
   publisher's name is nails on a chalkboard. So format
   your citations properly for the same reason you use
   the same font throughout your paper: to keep relatively meaningless details from being a distraction
   from what is important (your thesis). What do you
   want your readers to remember? Your inability to
   follow simple directions, or your thesis?

10. Plagiarize. If you aren't sure where the line is, ask. Show
    your professor your source and your paper, and ask. If
    you got an *idea* from a source, footnote it. If you got
    words from a source, put quotes around those words
    and footnote it. There is no shame in footnoting!

THEOLOGICAL RESEARCH AND WRITING TOOLS

THERE ARE FIVE BOOKS that you'll want to have available throughout your research and writing process. They are best used as references for when you come up against a particular question. The first three sources here are listed in go-to order for questions about formatting and style—if *The SBL Handbook of Style* doesn't answer your question, go to Turabian; if Turabian doesn't answer your question, go to *The Chicago Manual of Style.* The *SBL Handbook* (which, if you are doing any kind of degree program in theological studies, you must own) is exclusively about technical issues that are unique to our field: how to cite certain ancient sources, how to cite odd publications like commentaries, how to abbreviate various translations of ancient texts, how to type in Greek and Hebrew fonts (or transliterate Greek and Hebrew words) and so on. Turabian's volume is more generally geared toward all kinds of academic research and writing. It covers technical issues such as citation format, big-picture issues such as writing and revising initial drafts of your research paper, and stylistic issues like punctuation and spelling. *The Chicago Manual of Style* is basically Turabian on steroids—much more detail, many more specific examples and so on.

Booth and Vyhmeister are reference sources for the research and writing process: planning your work, engaging sources, making arguments, handling and presenting evidence and so on. As their respective titles make clear, Booth is geared toward any kind of academic research, while Vyhmeister targets a narrower constituency: students of religion and theology. Vyhmeister treats a host of somewhat randomly assembled topics such as "Research Reading," "Formatting the Paper," "The Case Study as Research" and "Doctor of Ministry Projects." Many of these discussions will be helpful to you at various points in your research process; if you have a question that is not addressed in this book (about *theological* research in particular), Vyhmeister is probably the best place to start looking for an answer.

Formatting and Style

Collins, Billie Jean, Bob Buller and John F. Kusko, eds. *The SBL Handbook of Style: For Biblical Studies and Related Disciplines*. 2nd ed. Atlanta: SBL Press, 2014.

Turabian, Kate L. *A Manual for Writers of Research Papers,*

Theses, and Dissertations. 8th ed. Revised by Wayne C. Booth, Gregory G. Colomb, Joseph M. Williams and the University of Chicago Press editorial staff. Chicago: University of Chicago Press, 2013.

University of Chicago Press. *The Chicago Manual of Style*. 16th ed. Chicago: University of Chicago Press, 2010.

Research and Writing Process

Booth, Wayne C., Gregory G. Colomb and Joseph M. Williams. *The Craft of Research*. 3rd ed. Chicago: University of Chicago Press, 2008.

Vyhmeister, Nancy Jean. *Your Guide to Writing Quality Research Papers: For Students of Religion and Theology*. 2nd ed. Grand Rapids: Zondervan, 2008.

Appendix C

SCHOLARLY RESOURCES FOR THEOLOGICAL RESEARCH

THE FOLLOWING IS A *partial* list of scholarly theological resources that you may find helpful in the research process. All of the journals listed are available through ATLA (though they are not necessarily all available in full-text PDF format). These lists are intended to offer general guidance; you may certainly find other helpful resources that are not included here.

PRIMARY SOURCES

As I discuss in the introduction, the array of translations and editions of some ancient texts can be overwhelming. The deeper you go, the more layers you will uncover! This list is not comprehensive but should cover the key texts you will regularly encounter in advanced undergraduate or graduate theological research.

Biblical texts. You probably already know that the Old Testament was originally written in Hebrew (with a little bit of Aramaic thrown in) and the New Testament was originally written in Greek. But here are two other bits of information you might not know: (1) there are numerous modern print versions of both the Hebrew OT and Greek NT to choose from, and (2) we've had Bible translators about as long as we've had Bibles, and ancient translations frequently serve as significant primary sources for certain kinds of theological research.

English Bibles. There's no right answer to this question—the simple fact is that there are lots of good translations of the Bible into English. The best advice I can give you, especially if you don't yet have the language skills to interact with Greek and Hebrew, is to use more than one translation in your research. If a critical piece of your argument depends on a nuance that appears in some translations but not others, especially if quite a different point is made by the wording of those others, ask your professor or check the standard commentaries on that text. Translation *is* interpretation, and Bible translators have to make interpretive decisions. Many of those decisions are easy, but some of them are difficult, and translation committees sometimes come to contrary conclusions at such points. If your argument requires that the NIV be right and the ESV be wrong on one of those difficult decisions, you need to have some idea of what the difficulty was and why your translation made the choice that it did.

Greek New Testament. All standard English translations of the New Testament are based on one or more of these. In research contexts, it's usually better to use the Nestle-Aland (NA) text, even though relatively few differences exist between the United Bible Societies (UBS) and NA editions. Ask your professor if they prefer the NA[27] or NA[28].

> *The Greek New Testament* (UBS[4]). 4th rev. ed. Stuttgart: Deutsche Bibelgesellschaft, 1983.
> *The Greek New Testament* (UBS[5]). 5th rev. ed. Stuttgart: Deutsche Bibelgesellschaft, 2014.
> *Novum Testamentum Graece* (NA[27]). 27th ed. Stuttgart: Deutsche Bibelgesellschaft, 1993.
> *Novum Testamentum Graece* (NA[28]). 28th ed. Stuttgart: Deutsche Bibelgesellschaft, 2012.

Greek Old Testament (Septuagint). No field in biblical studies offers more opportunities for exciting new research than that of the Greek Old Testament, often called the Septuagint or LXX. The only modern English translation of the LXX is the New English Translation of the Septuagint (NETS), while those seeking to read it in Greek have an accessible option (Rahlfs, in one relatively inexpensive volume), and two more comprehensive options (the Göttingen and Cambridge editions, each in twenty-plus very expensive volumes). Buy Rahlfs, and refer to the

Göttingen edition in the reference section of the library only if you are doing advanced graduate work or making an argument with a text-critical component (which requires use of the Göttingen textual apparatus). If you'd like more technical information than Rahlfs offers but in a book not yet published in the Göttingen series, check out the Cambridge edition, which reproduces a single ancient manuscript (Codex Vaticanus) along with notes on other manuscripts.

> *New English Translation of the Septuagint* (NETS). Edited by Albert Pietersma and Benjamin G. Wright. New York: Oxford University Press, 2009.[1]
>
> *The Old Testament in Greek According to the Text of Codex Vaticanus* (Cambridge). 9 vols. Edited by Alan E. Brooke, Norman McLean and Henry St John Thackeray. Cambridge: Cambridge University Press, 1906–1940.
>
> *Septuaginta: Editio altera* (Rahlfs). 2nd rev. ed. Edited by Alfred Rahlfs and Robert Hahnart. Göttingen: Deutsche Bibelgesellschaft, 2007.
>
> *Septuaginta. Vetus Testamentum Graecum. Auctoritate Academiae Scientiarum Göttingensis editum* (Göttingensis). 20 vols. Göttingen: Vandenhoeck & Ruprecht, 1931–.

---

[1]NETS is also available in a free PDF online: http://ccat.sas.upenn.edu /nets/edition.

Hebrew Old Testament. The *Biblia Hebraica* series has long been the standard scholarly edition of the Hebrew Old Testament. When scholars talk about the "Old Testament" or the "First Testament" or the "Hebrew Bible," this is usually the book they have in mind, and all English translations of the Old Testament (unless otherwise specified) are based on this text. The most current comprehensive version is *Biblia Hebraica Stuttgartensia* (BHS), while the *Biblia Hebraica Quinta* (BHQ), the most recent edition, is being released in pieces (each new volume includes one book or group of books from the Old Testament), and it will be years before the entire Old Testament is complete.[2] Purchase and use BHS (one volume) as your go-to text, and refer to BHQ if the text you're studying exists in that edition. If you are doing serious text-critical work especially, BHQ includes a vast amount of data not found in BHS and earlier editions.

> *Biblia Hebraica Quinta* (BHQ). Stuttgart: Deutsche Bibelgesellschaft, 2004–.
> *Biblia Hebraica Stuttgartensia* (BHS). Stuttgart: Deutsche Bibelgesellschaft, 1967–1977.

The Latin Bible (Vulgate). Saint Jerome (AD 340–420) translated the Old and New Testaments from Hebrew and

---

[2]Genesis, Deuteronomy, Judges, Proverbs, Ruth, Song of Songs, Ecclesiastes, Lamentations, Esther, Ezra, Nehemiah and the twelve "Minor Prophets" are available as of 2015 in the *BHQ* edition.

Greek into Latin; his translation became the common (*vulgata* = "the common one") Bible, as well as the authoritative one, for the Roman Catholic Church.

> Weber, Robertus, and Roger Gryson, eds. *Biblia Sacra: Iuxta Vulgatum Versionem*. Editionem quintam emandatam retractatam. Stuttgart: Deutsche Bibelgesellschaft, 2007.

Targums. The Targums (or Targumim) are a collection of Aramaic translations of the Old Testament (except Ezra, Nehemiah and Daniel) produced at various points in the Second Temple period and perhaps beyond. The most prominent Targumim are *Onqelos*/*Onkelos* (Tg. Onq.), *Pseudo-Jonathan* (TG. Ps.-J.), and *Neofiti*/*Neophyti* (Tg. Neof.). The go-to English translations appear in *The Aramaic Bible* (ArBib), while numerous original-language editions exist. I have listed the most recent and most frequently cited editions below.

> *The Aramaic Bible: The Targums* (ArBib). 22 vols. Collegeville, MN: Liturgical Press, 1992–.
> Klein, Michael L. *The Fragment-Targums of the Pentateuch According to Their Extant Sources*. 2 vols. AnBib 76. Rome: Biblical Institute Press, 1989.
> Klein, Michael L. *Genizah Manuscripts of Palestinian Targum to the Pentateuch*. 2 vols. Cincinnati: Hebrew Union College Press, 1986.

Rieder, David. *Pseudo-Jonathan: Targum Jonathan Ben Uziel on the Pentateuch*. Jerusalem: Salomon's, 1974.

Sperber, Alexander, ed. *The Bible in Aramaic Based on Old Manuscripts and Printed Texts 1–IVA*. Leiden: Brill, 1959–1968.

Samaritan Pentateuch. The Samaritan Pentateuch (SP) doesn't generate much interest outside the scholarly community, and even scholars tend to pay little or no attention to it. Readers of the New Testament often think of Samaritans as merely a group of half-Jews who were despised by "real" Jews (see Jn 4:9), and only recently was the first English translation of SP completed. Like its Hebrew counterpart, SP was also translated into Aramaic (thus the *Samaritan Targum of the Pentateuch* [Sam. Tg.]).

Tal, Abraham. *The Samaritan Targum of the Pentateuch: A Critical Edition* (Sam. Tg.). 3 vols. Tel-Aviv: Tel-Aviv University Press, 1980–1983.

Tal, Abraham, and Moshe Florentin, eds. *The Pentateuch: The Samaritan Version and the Masoretic Version*. Tel Aviv: Tel Aviv University Press, 2010.

Tsedaka, Benyamim and Sharon Sullivan. *The Israelite Samaritan Version of the Torah: First English Translation Compared with the Masoretic Version*. Grand Rapids: Eerdmans, 2013.

Syriac and Coptic. Serious students of the Old Testament and its reception may want to take a look at the Syriac and Coptic editions. The Syriac Old Testament appears in both Syriac and a standard English translation, while the Coptic exists only in the original. If you just can't rest until you know how the Coptic reads at a particular point, but now isn't the time to learn another language, ask your professor. If your professor doesn't read Coptic (even among biblical scholars, Coptic is not standard fare), he or she might know someone who does. During my dissertation research I wanted to know how a single line in Exodus 19:13 read in the Coptic version, so I emailed a former professor who I thought might be able to point me in the right direction. He then contacted a couple of his colleagues in the Near Eastern Languages and Cultures department at UCLA, who emailed me a translation of the line I was examining.[3] Such is the beauty of the scholarly community!

> Koster, M. D., and The Peshitta Institute, eds. *The Old Testament in Syriac According to the Peshitta Version.* Leiden: Brill, 1972–.
>
> Peters, Melvin K. H., ed. *A Critical Edition of the Coptic (Bohairic) Pentateuch.* 5 vols. Atlanta: Scholars Press, 1983–1986.

---

[3]Always give credit where credit is due. In my dissertation the following footnote appears connected to the line in question: "Thanks to Joseph Sanzo and Hany Takla of the University of California at Los Angeles for the translation."

Weitzman, Michael P. *The Syriac Version of the Old Testament.* University of Cambridge Oriental Publications 56. Cambridge: Cambridge University Press, 1999.

Dead Sea Scrolls (DSS).[4] You probably already know the story: in 1947 a shepherd in the wilderness east of Jerusalem went into a cave looking for a lost sheep and accidentally made the greatest archaeological discovery of the twentieth century. In that cave, as well as others in the area, were thousands of scrolls and fragments of scrolls, dating as early as the second century BC, including copies of almost every book in the Old Testament as well as dozens of other documents. Several reliable and inexpensive English translations exist, of which I have listed the two most common. The standard scholarly edition is the Discoveries in the Judean Desert series (DJD), though more recent editions of some texts have appeared in the newer Princeton series edited by James Charlesworth, which (unlike DJD) includes both a critical text and English translation.

The Dead Sea Scrolls: Hebrew, Aramaic, and Greek Texts with English Translations. The Princeton

---

[4]Note that the DSS contain many biblical and nonbiblical scrolls, so technically this set belongs both in this category and in the "Jewish and Greco-Roman Texts" portion below.

Theological Seminary Dead Sea Scrolls Project. 10 vols. Tübingen: Mohr Siebeck, 1991–.

Discoveries in the Judean Desert Series (DJD). 40 vols. Oxford: Clarendon and Oxford University Press, 1955–2010.

Martinez, Florentino G. *The Dead Sea Scrolls Translated: The Qumran Texts in English.* 2nd ed. Grand Rapids: Eerdmans, 1996.

Wise, Michael O., Martin G. Abegg and Edward M. Cook. *The Dead Sea Scrolls: A New Translation.* San Francisco: HarperSanFrancisco, 1996.

Ancient Near Eastern, Jewish and Greco-Roman Texts. Biblical and early Christian authors did not write in cultural and literary vacuums; their writings emerged from real historical situations alongside vast quantities of other literature. In this section you'll find out how to access the surviving pieces of that other contemporary literature in order to understand the historical context out of which the Bible emerged.

Ancient Near Eastern texts. The term *ancient Near Eastern* refers, generally speaking, to Israel and its neighbors (Persia, Babylon, Ugarit, Egypt, etc.) before the time of Alexander the Great (mid–fourth century BC). If you are researching the history, language, culture and religion of Israel in the Old Testament period, this is where you find your nonbiblical primary sources. A few of these texts you may have heard of, like Enuma Elish and the Epic of Gilgamesh. But as you've probably realized by now, the texts you hear about in class are only the tip of the iceberg of the resources out there. Each of the sets below cuts a wide swath through the primary sources of the ancient Near East, though none is comprehensive.

> Hallo, William W., and K. Lawson Younger, eds. *The Context of Scripture*. 3 vols. Leiden: Brill, 1997–2003.
>
> Kitchen, Kenneth A., and Paul J. N. Lawrence, eds. *Treaty, Law and Covenant in the Ancient Near East*. 3 vols. Wiesbaden: Harrassowitz, 2012.
>
> Lewis, Theodore J., ed. Writings from the Ancient World Series. Atlanta: Scholars/SBL Press, 1990–.
>
> Pritchard, James B., ed. *The Ancient Near East: An Anthology of Texts and Pictures*. Princeton, NJ: Princeton University Press, 1958.

Loeb Classical Library. Have you ever noticed a wall of small green and red volumes in the reference section of your library? That is the Loeb Classical Library (LCL), the largest existing collection of primary sources from the Greco-Roman era. Plato, Aristotle, Cicero, Josephus, Philo, you name it—they're all here. Every volume is a diglot, which means that when you open one of the books, you will see the original language printed on the left and the English translation printed on the right. The green volumes are Greek authors and the red volumes are Latin authors. A word of caution: while the series has been accumulating since 1911, volumes are retranslated every few decades, so make sure you have the most recent edition.

> Loeb Classical Library (LCL). Cambridge, MA: Harvard University Press. 1911–.

Pseudepigrapha. One of the most valuable tools for studying the reception of the Old Testament and the context of the New Testament is the *Old Testament Pseudepigrapha (OTP).*[5] *Pseudepigrapha* ("false writings") is a term used to describe texts that claim to be written by someone other than their actual author. *Old Testament Pseudepigrapha* refers to a corpus of writings claiming to be written by prominent Old Testament figures (Moses, Enoch, Abraham, Solomon, etc.). The "Animal Apocalypse" in *1 Enoch* happens to be a personal favorite—think Revelation meets George Orwell's *Animal Farm.*

> *The Old Testament Pseudepigrapha (OTP).* 2 vols. Edited by James H. Charlesworth. Peabody, MA: Hendrickson, 1983.

---

[5]Some *OTP* texts were written well after the time of the NT and may have been written or edited under Christian influence. Make sure you read the introductions to each text before you make any assumptions about their dates in relation to the NT. For a more extensive listing of primary editions see the somewhat-dated-but-still-useful *Introduction to the Talmud and Midrash* by H. L. Strack and G. Stemberger.

> *Old Testament Pseudepigrapha: More Noncanonical Scriptures.* 2 vols. Edited by Richard Bauckham, James R. Davila and Alexander Panayotov. Grand Rapids: Eerdmans, 2013–.

Rabbinic texts.[6] Rabbinic Jewish texts vary in importance depending on what you plan to do with them. If you want to understand Rabbinic Judaism, their importance goes without saying. If you want to follow the variegated path of the reception of the Old Testament, they are invaluable. If you want to understand Jewish perspectives in the time of the New Testament, things get a little complicated. The basic issue is this: first, few or none of the sources that fall into this category (Mishnah, Talmud and so on) can be dated with any certainty from any earlier than the end of the second century AD (100–150 years after the writing of the New Testament). Second, the destruction of Jerusalem and the temple in AD 70 changes the practice of Judaism in ways that are difficult to overestimate. So, for example, we simply cannot be sure that the Mishnah (late second/early third century AD) shows us a strand of Judaism that existed when Paul wrote Galatians (AD 40s or 50s). All this to say: read Rabbinic texts, but be wary of using them

---

[6]The term *rabbinic Judaism* typically refers to the mainline strand of Jewish faith and practice that emerged following the destruction of the temple in AD 70 and persisted through the medieval period.

as primary sources when doing New Testament studies, and always pay close attention to the dating for each individual source.

Primary Texts:

The Babylonian Talmud. Edited by Isidore Epstein. 30 vols. London: Soncino, 1965–1989.

Mekilta de-Rabbi Ishmael. Edited by Jacob Z. Lauterbach. 3 vols. Philadelphia: The Jewish Publication Society of America, 1933.

Midrash Rabbah. Edited by Harry Freedman and Maurice Simon. 10 vols. London: Soncino, 1992.

The Mishnah: Translated from the Hebrew with Introduction and Brief Explanatory Notes. Edited by Herbert Danby. Oxford: Oxford University Press: 1933.

Pěsiḳta dě-Rab Kahăna. Edited by William G. Braude and Israel J. Kapstein. Philadelphia: JPS, 1975.

Pěsiḳta Rabbati: Discourses for Feasts, Fasts, and Special Sabbaths. Edited by William G. Braude. Yale Judaica Series 18. New Haven, CT: Yale University Press, 1968.

Sifra: The Rabbinic Commentary on Leviticus (An American Translation). Edited by Jacob Neusner and Roger Brooks. Atlanta: Scholars Press, 1985.

Sifré to Numbers: An American Translation and Explanation. 2 vols. Edited by Jacob Neusner. Brown Judaic Studies 118. Atlanta: Scholars Press, 1986.

Sifré to Deuteronomy: An Analytical Translation. 2 vols. Edited by Jacob Neusner. Brown Judaic Studies 98. Atlanta: Scholars Press, 1987.

Sifré: A Tannaitic Commentary on Deuteronomy. Edited by Reuven Hammer. Yale Judaica Series 24. New Haven, CT: Yale University Press, 1986.

The Talmud of the Land of Israel: A Preliminary Translation and Explanation. Edited by Jacob Neusner. 35 vols. Chicago: University of Chicago Press, 1982–1993.

The Tosefta. Edited by Jacob Neusner and Richard S. Sarason. 6 vols. New York: Ktav, 1977–1986.

Anthologies:

The Book of Legends (Sefer ha-Aggadah): Legends from the Talmud and Midrash. Edited by Hayyim N. Bialik, Yehoshua H. Ravnitzki and William G. Braude. New York: Schocken, 1992.

Cohen, Menachem, ed. *Mikra'ot Gedolot Haketer: A Revised and Augmented Scientific Edition of "Mikra'ot Gedolot" Based on the Aleppo Codex and Early Medieval MSS.* 23 vols. Bar-Ilan University Press, 2010–.[7]

Ginzberg, Louis. *The Legends of the Jews.* 7 vols. Philadelphia: Jewish Publication Society, 1909–1938.

---

[7]In Hebrew. Some volumes have appeared in an English translation by Michael Carasik called *The Commentator's Bible* (Philadelphia: JPS, 2005–).

> Kasher, Menahem M. *Encyclopedia of Biblical Interpretation: A Millennial Anthology*. Translated by Harry Freedman. 10 vols. New York: American Biblical Encyclopedia Society, 1953–1979.

Early Christian Texts. Many prominent figures in early Christianity have received sufficient attention to merit scholarly editions of their primary texts that exist as stand-alone volumes. In this section I have simply listed the major collections of such literature for students who want to get started off on the right foot. If you are doing major research on a particular figure or text, you should always check with your professor to see if he or she prefers a particular edition of your primary sources. See Johannes Quasten, *Patrology*, 4 vols. (Westminster, MD: Newman, 1950–1960), for more extensive lists of primary text editions.

Collections in English. Several reliable English editions of various early Christian writings exist, and it is difficult to say whether one is more reliable than the other. A few primary texts exist in more than one of the series listed below; if you come across such a text I recommend asking your professor's opinion on the best available option. (Many early Christian and theological sources have no SBL abbreviation; I have used the abbreviations identified by the series themselves.)

Ancient Christian Writers Series (ACW). New York: Paulist, 1946–.

The Ante-Nicene Fathers (ANF). 10 vols. Edited by A. Alexander Coxe. 1885–1887. Repr., Peabody, MA: Hendrickson, 1994.[8]

Elliot, James K. *The Apocryphal New Testament: A Collection of Apocryphal Christian Literature in an English Translation*. Rev. ed. Oxford: Clarendon, 1993.[9]

The Fathers of the Church: A New Translation (FC). 130 vols. Washington, DC: Catholic University of America Press, 1947–.

Fathers of the Church (Medieval Continuation) (FCM). 15 vols. Washington, DC: Catholic University of America Press, 1989–.

Holmes, Michael W. *The Apostolic Fathers* (AF). 3rd ed. Grand Rapids: Baker Academic, 2007.[10]

Meyer, Marvin W. *The Nag Hammadi Scriptures: The Revised and Updated Translation of Sacred Gnostic Texts*. New York: HarperCollins, 2009.[11]

---

[8]Just to be clear: "ante" Nicene means *before* Nicea, not *against* it.

[9]Note the difference between the Apocrypha, a group of texts found in the Septuagint and placed between the Old Testament and New Testament in modern Catholic and Orthodox Bibles, and the New Testament Apocrypha, a group of texts originating in or around early Christianity that are not included in any canon.

[10]This volume is a diglot: Greek on one page and English on the other.

[11]Some will question the inclusion of this volume in the category of Christian texts. But if you are interested in how early Christianity

The Nicene and Post-Nicene Fathers (*NPNF¹*). First
   series. 14 vols. Edited by Philip Shaff. 1886–1889.
   Repr., Peabody, MA: Hendrickson, 1994.
The Nicene and Post-Nicene Fathers (*NPNF²*). Second
   Series. 14 vols. Edited by Philip Schaff and Henry
   Wace. Repr., Peabody, MA: Hendrickson, 1996.
Oxford Early Christian Texts (OECT). 19 vols.
   Oxford: Oxford University Press, 1971–2015.
Popular Patristics Series (PPS). 51 vols. Crestwood,
   NY: St. Vladimir's Seminary Press, 1997–.
Schneemelcher, Wilhelm. *New Testament Apoc-*
   rypha. 2 vols. Translated by R. McL. Wilson.
   Philadelphia: Westminster, 1963–1966.
Sources of Early Christian Thought (SECT). 5 vols.
   Minneapolis: Augsburg Fortress, 1980–1981.

Greek and Latin Texts. Before you get excited and jump
into the deep end, you need to know one thing: none of
the sources listed below have any English in them. None.
No English translations, no English introductions, no
English tables of contents, nothing. Just so you know what
you're getting yourself into! Unless your class has a specific
language prerequisite, you will certainly not be expected
to deal with these texts. But if you're doing advanced

---

interacted with its religious context and morphed into various forms,
some of which ultimately merit the term *Christian* and some of which
do not, the Gnostic literature fits into your primary texts category.

graduate work in early Christianity or are comfortable reading Greek, Latin or French, working from these editions whenever possible is a must.

Sources Chrétiennes (SC) is an extensive collection of early Christian texts (sermons, letters, commentaries, etc.) in diglot form—French on one side and Greek or Latin on the other. If your Greek and Latin are mediocre or nonexistent but your French is solid, this is the way to go. Of those listed here, this is the most user-friendly and the most likely to be in your library.

The other two sets here are for the really ambitious. J.-P. Migne compiled the largest collection in existence of original-language early and medieval church texts, the Patrologia Latina (PL) and Patrologia Graeca (PG). No modern edition of these collections exists, nor any translation, so only more serious theological libraries are likely to have a copy. Some libraries are willing to lend them through interlibrary loan, so there's hope even if your library doesn't have the set. The entire set contains about 390 volumes, but each one contains as much (in terms of word count) as nine or ten LCL volumes due to small margins, small print, large pages and thick volumes.

Updated editions of some of the works in PG and PL have been appearing periodically in the Corpus Christianorum, another large exclusively original-language collection of early Christian literature.

Corpus Christianorum: Continuatio Mediaevalis/ Series Graeca/Series Latina (CCCM/CCSG/ CCSL). Turnhout: Brepols, 1953–.

Migne, J.-P, ed. Patrologiae Cursus Completus: Series Graeca/Series Latina (PG/PL). 1844–1866.

Sources Chrétiennes (SC). Paris: Les Éditions du Cerf. 1941–.

STANDARD TERTIARY SOURCES

Alexander, T. Desmond, Brian S. Rosner and Robert Yarbrough, eds. *New Dictionary of Biblical Theology.* Downers Grove, IL: IVP Academic, 2000.

Alexander, T. Desmond, and David Baker, eds. *Dictionary of the Old Testament: Pentateuch.* Downers Grove, IL: IVP Academic, 2003.

Arnold, Bill T., and H.G.M. Williamson, eds. *Dictionary of the Old Testament: Historical Books.* Downers Grove, IL: IVP Academic, 2005.

Davids, Peter H., and Ralph P. Martin, eds. *Dictionary of the Later New Testament and its Developments.* Downers Grove, IL: IVP Academic, 1997.

Enns, Peter, and Tremper Longman III, eds. *Dictionary of the Old Testament: Wisdom, Poetry, and Writings.* Downers Grove, IL: IVP Academic, 2008.

Evans, Craig A., and Stanley E. Porter, eds. *Dictionary of New Testament Background.* Downers Grove, IL: IVP Academic, 2000.

Freedman, David Noel, ed. *Anchor Bible Dictionary.* 6 v.
    New York: Doubleday, 1992.

Green, Joel B., Jeannine K. Brown and Nicholas Perrin,
    eds. *Dictionary of Jesus and the Gospels.* 2nd ed.
    Downers Grove, IL: IVP Academic, 2013.

Hawthorne, Gerald, Ralph P. Martin and Daniel G. Reid,
    eds. *Dictionary of Paul and His Letters.* Downers Grove,
    IL: IVP Academic, 1993.

Sakenfeld, Katherine Doob, Samuel E. Balentine and Brian
    K. Blount, eds. *The New Interpreter's Dictionary of the
    Bible.* 5 vols. Nashville: Abingdon, 2006.

Vanhoozer, Kevin J., ed. *Dictionary for Theological Interpre-
    tation of the Bible.* Grand Rapids: Baker Academic, 2005.

Webster, John B., Kathryn Tanner and Ian Torrance, eds.
    Oxford Handbook of Systematic Theology. New York:
    Oxford University Press, 2007.

What Are They Saying About . . . ? Series. New York:
    Paulist, 1977–2006.

MAJOR SCHOLARLY PUBLISHERS FOR THEOLOGICAL STUDIES

The names of publishers printed in their books sometimes change from year to year: Fortress = Augsburg Fortress, J. C. B. Mohr (Paul Siebeck) = Mohr Siebeck, Editrice Pontificio Institutio Biblico = Pontifical Biblical
Institute, and so on. When you document a book in your
research bibliography, record the publisher as it is given

that particular volume. Various university presses also belong on a list like this, especially Cambridge, Oxford, Yale, Harvard, Indiana, Chicago, Notre Dame, Louvain/Leuven and Baylor.

Abingdon
Baker Books/Baker
    Academic
Brazos Press
Brill
Broadman & Holman
Catholic Biblical
    Association of America
Crossway
Doubleday
Éditions du Cerf
Editrice Pontificio
    Instituto Biblico
Eerdmans
Eisenbrauns
Fortress
Harper & Row
Hendrickson
InterVarsity Press/IVP
    Academic
Jewish Publication Society
JSOT Press
Ktav
Liturgical Press
Mercer
Mohr Siebeck
Neukirchener
Paternoster
Paulist Press
Peeters
Pickwick
Pilgrim
Prebyterian & Reformed
Routledge
Scholars Press
SCM Press
Sheffield Academic Press
SBL Press
SPCK
T&T Clark
University Press of America
Vandenhoeck & Ruprecht
Walter de Gruyter
Westminster John Knox
Wipf & Stock
Zondervan

SCHOLARLY JOURNALS
(WITH STANDARD ABBREVIATIONS)

Don't be intimidated by the French and German journals listed here—they frequently contain articles in English.

Andrews University Seminary Studies (*AUSS*)

Anglican Theological Review (*AThR*)

Biblica (*Bib*)

Biblical Interpretation (*BibInt*)

Biblical Theology Bulletin (*BTB*)

Bibliotheca Sacra (*BSac*)

Biblische Zeitschrift (*BZ*)

Bulletin for Biblical Research (*BBR*)

Bulletin of the American Schools of Oriental Research (*BASOR*)

Bulletin of the International Organization for Septuagint and Cognate Studies (*BIOSCS*)

Calvin Theological Journal (*CTJ*)

Catholic Biblical Quarterly (*CBQ*)

Concordia Journal (CJ)

Concordia Theological Monthly (*CTM*)

Concordia Theological Quarterly (*CTQ*)

Currents in Biblical Research (*CurBR*)

Dead Sea Discoveries (*DSD*)

Dialog (*Di*)

Ephemerides Theologicae Lovanienses (*ETL*)

European Journal of Theology (*EuroJTh*)

Evangelical Quarterly (*EvQ*)

Ex Auditu (ExAud)
Expository Times (ExpTim)
Hebrew Annual Review (HAR)
Hebrew Union College Annual (HUCA)
Heythrop Journal (HeyJ)
Horizons in Biblical Theology (HBT)
International Journal of Systematic Theology (IJST)
Interpretation (Int)
Jewish Bible Quarterly (JBQ)
Journal for the Study of Judaism in the Persian, Hellenistic,
    and Roman Periods (JSJ)
Journal for the Study of the New Testament (JSNT)
Journal for the Study of the Old Testament (JSOT)
Journal for the Study of Paul and His Letters (JSPL)
Journal of Biblical Literature (JBL)
Journal of Greco-Roman Christianity and Judaism (JGRChJ)
Journal of Religion (JR)
Journal of the Adventist Theological Society (JATS)
Journal of the American Academy of Religion (JAAR)
Journal of the Evangelical Theological Society (JETS)
Journal of Theological Interpretation (JTI)
Journal of Theological Studies (JTS)
Lexington Theological Quarterly (LTQ)
Literature and Theology (LT)
Lutheran Quarterly (LQ)
Lutheran Theological Journal (LTJ)
Neotestamentica (Neot)

New Testament Studies (NTS)

Novum Testamentum (NovT)

Perspectives in Religious Studies (PRSt)

Pro Ecclesia (ProEccl)

Restoration Quarterly (ResQ)

Review and Expositor (RevExp)

Revue biblique (RB)

Revue de Qumran (RevQ)

Scottish Bulletin of Evangelical Theology (SBET)

Scottish Journal of Theology (SJT)

Semeia (Semeia)

Society of Biblical Literature Seminar Papers (SBLSP)

Southern Baptist Journal of Theology (SBJT)

Southwestern Journal of Theology (SwJT)

St. Vladimir's Theological Quarterly (SVTQ)

Studies in Biblical Theology (SBT)

Theological Studies (TS)

Trinity Journal (TJ)

Tyndale Bulletin (TynBul)

Vetus Testamentum (VT)

Westminster Theological Journal (WTJ)

Zeitschrift für die alttestamentliche Wissenschaft (ZAW)

Zeitschrift für die neuetestamentliche Wissenschaft und die Kunde der älteren Kirche (ZNW)

SCHOLARLY COMMENTARY SERIES

Anchor Bible Commentary

Ancient Christian Commentary on Scripture

Baker Exegetical Commentary on the New Testament

Brazos Theological Commentary on the Bible

Catholic Commentary on Sacred Scripture

Hermeneia Commentary Series

International Critical Commentary

IVP New Testament Commentary

New American Commentary

New Cambridge Bible Commentary

New Century Bible

New International Bible Commentary

New International Commentary on the New Testament

New International Commentary on the Old Testament

New International Greek Testament Commentary

New Testament Library

Pillar New Testament Commentary

Sacra Pagina New Testament Commentary

Two Horizons New Testament Commentary

Two Horizons Old Testament Commentary

Tyndale Old Testament Commentary

Word Biblical Commentary

Zondervan Exegetical Commentary on the New Testament

Appendix D

NAVIGATING THE ATLA RELIGION DATABASE

THE ATLA RELIGION DATABASE should be accessible to you through your library website. Once you find the main ATLA link, you should now see a page that looks like figure D.1.

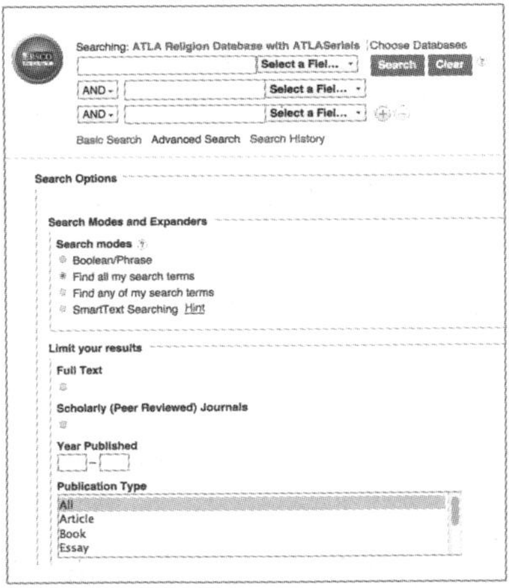

Figure D.1.

The first thing you should do on this page is to set your search options. First, click the "Scholarly (Peer Reviewed) Journals" box in the left column. Second, click on "Article," "Book" and "Essay" under the "Publication Type" list (unless your primary source is a recent publication, in which case, click "Book Reviews" as well). Third, select "English" from the language list (unless you are comfortable with other languages, especially German or French). These steps will eliminate a large number of unnecessary sources that will make the search process more tedious. See the example in figure D.2.

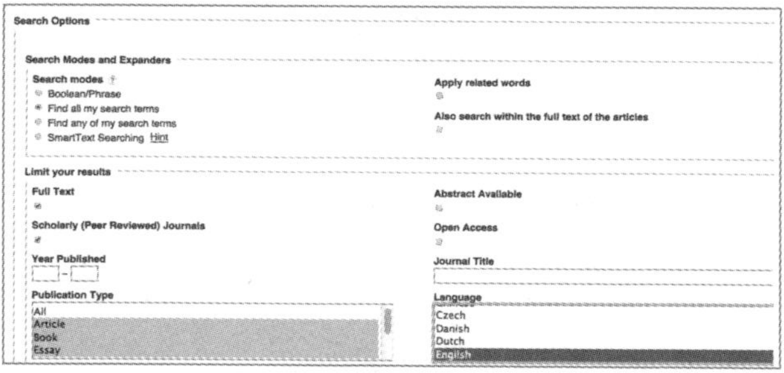

Figure D.2.

Another step you may want to take is to click on the "Full Text" box in the left column. This will set your search to only list sources that are available in full-text format through ATLA (usually a PDF), eliminating the need to go to the journal stacks in your library. This can be helpful when you make your initial foray into the scholarship on your issue. However, *do not assume that every article you need will be available in full text.* You must visit the journal stacks at some point, but choosing the full-text option at the beginning can make your initial search simpler.

Now you're ready to begin searching. Type in your broad topic ("New Testament" is too broad; "kingdom of God" and "Mark" are sufficiently narrow at this point). You do not need to worry about the "select a field" option right now. When I hit the search button, I came up with fifty-six options.

Here you can see the top three hits (see figure D.3).[1] The first hit (about the resurrection) *could* be relevant, but it isn't *obviously* so. The latter two are more promising—one about opponents of the kingdom of God in a single text,

Figure D.3.

---

[1]By the time this book is in print, the top three hits will probably have changed due to more recent scholarship and programming adjustments made by the search engine. For what it's worth, I've had to redo this screenshot and rewrite this paragraph three or four times since I first ran the search in the early stage of writing back in 2009. So if you run this same search and the results don't look exactly the same as what you see here, don't be alarmed.

and the other about how Mark calls us to engage the kingdom of God. Since I ran this search after I had narrowed my topic to "opposition to the kingdom of God in Mark," the second article by Kelly Iverson about the parable of the wicked tenants was the one I certainly needed to download and engage more thoroughly. Fifty-six hits on this type of search is a good sign; that's a very reasonable number of articles to scan through, but not so few that you need to reword your search.

It never hurts to retry the search with slightly different terms—"kingdom" instead of "kingdom of God," "Mark's Gospel" instead of "Mark," and so on. Search engines are funny things, and you want to make sure you don't miss an obvious source because you didn't use just the right wording. You can also change your search fields. Searching for your terms in "TX all text" will usually not get you very far unless you have very specific terms. "Mark" and "kingdom of God" are far too common—this search yields 13,280 hits!

You can also search for your terms using the "SU Subjects" field. This search for "kingdom of God" and "Mark" offers twenty-six results, some of which have the potential to be useful for my research. However, you'll notice that some of the useful sources that popped up in my original search do not appear here, so it would have been a mistake to jump immediately to the "SU Subjects" field. If you get too many results on the first search, this can be a good next step.

Once you've found some articles that may be useful for your research, you can download them. Click on the "PDF Full Text" link below the article description and save the file to your computer.

ZOTERO BIBLIOGRAPHY SOFTWARE

BIBLIOGRAPHY SOFTWARE is one of the greatest provisions to theological research (and other kinds of research!) of the modern era. My personal favorite is Zotero, so I'll walk you through installing, setting up and using the program.

INSTALLATION (WORKS WITH MAC, WINDOWS AND LINUX OPERATING SYSTEMS)

Go to zotero.org. Zotero comes in two forms: as a Firefox add-on or as a standalone application. I recommend the standalone version. Note that you'll have to download a separate browser extension if you choose this option.[1] All three of these downloads are accessible from the main download page.

---

[1]When you're installing the browser extension, make sure you select yes when you are asked if you want Zotero Standalone and Firefox to share the same library.

CREATING ENTRIES

Once you have downloaded the program and opened it, you should see a screen that looks like figure E.1. Now for the fun part—entering sources of every shape and size into your research bibliography. There are two ways to do this: manually and through your web browser.

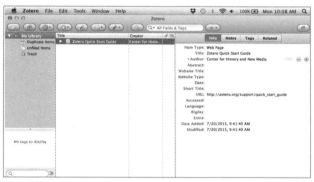

Figure E.1.

Manual entry. First, click the green plus sign and select the type of source you want to enter. Different kinds of sources (commentaries, journal articles, etc.) have some unique bibliographic features. I've chosen a journal article to illustrate the process (see figure E.2).

Next, enter the necessary information step by step (see figure E.3). You'll notice a couple of things about this entry. First, you have to enter the information correctly for it to show up correctly in your footnotes and bibliography. If you misspell a word in your entry, Zotero isn't going to

Figure E.2.

autocorrect it. Second, you have to enter all the necessary information. For a journal article, that means title, publication, volume, issue, year, journal abbreviation and short title.[2] The short title is the one that will show up in your footnotes after your initial citation of a source. So, for example, Ford Battles's essay "God Was Accommodating Himself to Human Capacity" was cited earlier in this book, so if I were to cite it again here, it would show up in an abbreviated form in the footnote.[3] Third, there are a couple of things you *don't* have to do manually. You don't italicize the name of the journal, and you don't enter any

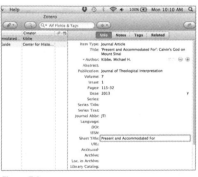

Figure E.3.

---

[2]See *The SBL Handbook of Style* (discussed in appendix B) for the necessary citation components of other kinds of sources.
[3]Battles, "God Was Accommodating Himself," 26.

punctuation outside the name of the article itself.

Web browser download. A second and sometimes simpler way to collect sources in your Zotero bibliography is through your web browser. Certain websites (your school library website is the best place to do this, since the information found there is almost certainly reliable) can send your Zotero library the information automatically and so save you some typing.

I'll use a commentary as an example. Let's say you are researching a text or topic in Romans and plan to use Douglas Moo's major commentary on that book. You search for it in your library's online database. Once you've got the book in your sights, click the small blue icon on the right side of your address bar (see figure E.4).

You'll see a small message pop up at the bottom right-hand of your screen that says "Saving to My Library," and now your library should look like figure E.5.

Notice that the information imported is not entirely correct (this will vary greatly depending on the website and the particular source you are putting into your Zotero library). First, the author's middle initial needs a period after it (J.). Second, no series is listed (in this case, the New International Commentary on the New Testament, or NICNT). Some websites will give you this, and some won't. Third, the "Place" and "Publisher" descriptions aren't quite right. Larger cities don't need the state or country listed, and even if you do need the state,

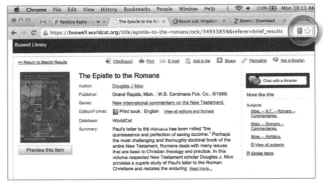

Figure E.4.

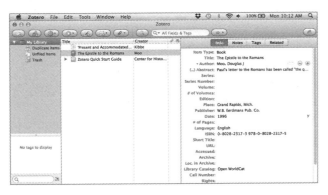

Figure E.5.

it should be in two-letter abbreviated form ("MI" not "Mich."). And the publisher is simply "Eerdmans." It also lacks a short title, which for commentaries should most often be simply the name of the book.

ORGANIZING

As your research bibliography grows, you'll need to keep it organized. Start by creating separate folders for different projects. Right-click on the "My Library" tab and choose "New Collection." Err on the side of being too narrow in your folder descriptions rather than too broad; you can always combine folders, but it's tough once you've got a few dozen or a few hundred entries in a folder to go through and manually divvy them up into smaller groups. For example, I have a large folder simply called "Hebrews" that contains several subfolders ("Use of the OT," "sacrifice/atonement" and so on). If you have sources that are likely to pop up again and again in different research settings (e.g., large one-volume dictionaries), put them in a separate folder for easy access. I also recommend making a separate folder for primary sources. The longer you use Zotero, the more complex your library will become. You want the navigation process to be as simple as possible.

CHOOSING STYLES

Once you begin writing your paper, you'll want to cite sources as you go along. The beauty of Zotero is that you don't need to interrupt your train of thought while writing to make sure you've put your citations in the proper format (this can get really complicated!). If you've entered the information properly the first time, you'll never have to worry about it again. The other thing you have to do is choose the proper style. There are several different ways to format footnotes, even within the theological disciplines. Sometimes it matters that you choose the right one; other times it simply matters that you pick one and stick with it. More than likely, your professor will want you to use the guidelines spelled out in *The SBL Handbook of Style*, so I'll illustrate this process using that one.

1. Click the gray wheel icon along the top bar of your Zotero program and select "Preferences" (see figure E.6).

2. Under that menu select "Cite" and "Styles," then click "Get Additional Styles" below the list that appears (see figure E.7).

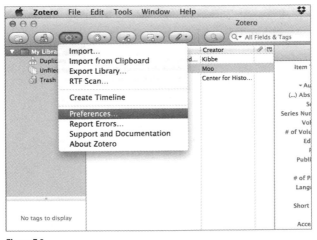

Figure E.6.

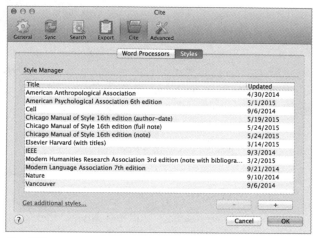

Figure E.7.

3. Your default web browser will take you to a list of style options; choose "Society of Biblical Literature 2nd edition (full note)" (see figure E.8).

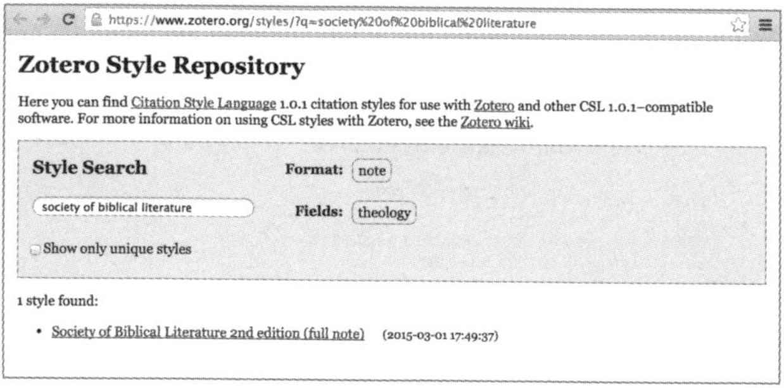

Figure E.8.

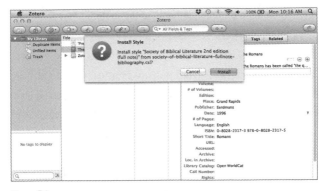

Figure E.9.

4. Install the SBL style (see figure E.9).

5. Select it and click OK in the style preferences menu (see figure E.10).

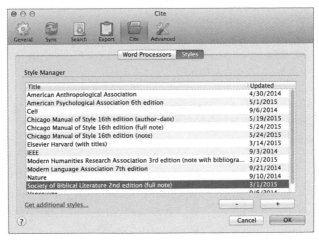

Figure E.10.

CREATING FOOTNOTES IN WORD

Let's say you either cite or depend on Moo's commentary on Romans for a particular point. Place your cursor at the very end of that sentence (avoid putting footnotes in the middle of a sentence if you can manage it), and click the scroll icon on your word processor menu bar. Select "Zotero" and "Add Citation" (see figure E.11). A red bar should appear (see figure E.12).

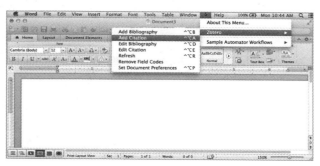

Figure E.11.

Figure E.12.

Enter in the name of either the author or the work (whichever will give you a shorter list) and click the proper source (see figure E.13). Type a comma, then the page number(s) you are citing. Both should disappear. This

Figure E.13.

indicates they have been pulled into the citation. See figure E.14. Hit enter, and your footnote should appear precisely where your cursor was, properly formatted.[4]

Figure E.14.

CREATING BIBLIOGRAPHIES

When you're done writing your paper—and I mean *done*— you need to insert your bibliography. The lingering question at this point is whether you will include all of the sources actually cited in your footnotes, or all of the sources you used in your research, whether or not they appear in a footnote in your paper. I recommend the first option, though you should ask your professor if they have a preference. I'll show you both ways just in case.

If your bibliography includes only those sources actually referenced in the paper, this is *really* easy. Put your cursor on the last page of your document, go back to the scroll icon and select "Add Bibliography" (see figure E.15).

---

[4]Douglas J. Moo, *The Epistle to the Romans*, NICNT (Grand Rapids: Eerdmans, 1996), 138.

Voíla! You have a bibliography. Read through it a couple of times, carefully, to spot formatting errors. The plain truth is that you were not as careful as you thought you were when you put the data into Zotero, so there are bound to be spelling errors, missing information and

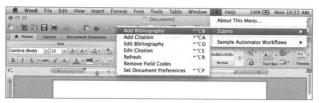

Figure E.15.

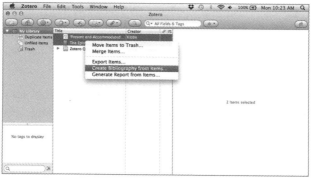

Figure E.16.

other problems. And don't forget that if you find an error here, the same error is going to show up back in the footnote where that particular source was cited.

The other way to create a bibliography is to copy and

paste it from Zotero itself. Perhaps you simply want to print your research bibliography, or you want to show your research beyond the sources that were actually cited in your paper. In this case you'll highlight the sources you want (if you need sources from more than one folder, combine them in a new folder first), right-click, and select "Create Bibliography from Items" (see figure E.16). Select the proper citation style and select "Bibliography" and "Copy to Clipboard" (see figure E.17). Now paste it in your Word processor. Once again, your bibliography will magically appear, with all the relevant information in proper formatting (assuming you entered it properly in the first place). Wasn't that easy?

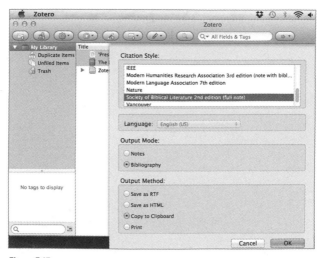

Figure E.17.

A SUGGESTED TIMELINE FOR THEOLOGICAL RESEARCH PAPERS

Good research takes time. How much time? It depends on a lot of factors: how big the paper is, how broad the assigned topic is, how much you know about the topic prior to the course, how long your term is and so on. What I've given you here is a suggestion for your research timeline that will vary depending on all these factors. At the very least this will give you something to work with. Assuming a sixteen-week course, something like the following should put you in good position to write a solid research paper.

- Weeks 1–6: Do your homework.

- Weeks 7–8: Start keeping your ears open to possible research topics. If something catches your attention, make a note of it for later, or begin working through step one ("Finding Direction").

- Week 9 (or the beginning of the second half of the

semester, depending on where fall/spring break happens): Complete step one ("Finding Direction").

- Weeks 10–13: Complete steps two ("Gathering Sources") and three ("Understanding Issues"). Note that these combined steps will take the majority of your time. There's no substitute for careful reading of primary and secondary sources.

- Weeks 14: Complete step four ("Understanding Issues"), with occasional steps back into steps two and three as necessary.

- Week 15: Complete step five ("Entering Discussion"). Write a rough draft and use that draft to identify weaknesses in your *research*. Go back to steps two through four as necessary. Once you feel that your research is complete, edit your paper for organization, grammar and so on. The sequence here is important: there's nothing more frustrating than spending hours on a section of your paper, honing each word until it sparkles with linguistic precision and rhetorical flourish, only to realize that further research reveals major shortcomings in its argument. Get the research done first, then hone the style.

ABOUT THE AUTHOR

Michael Kibbe (PhD, Wheaton College) is assistant professor of Bible at Moody Bible Institute (Spokane) in Spokane, Washington, where he teaches Greek and hermeneutics. He is the author of *Godly Fear or Ungodly Failure? Hebrews 12 and the Sinai Theophanies* and has published articles in *Journal of Theological Studies*, *Biblica*, *Journal of Theological Interpretation* and *Journal for the Study of Paul and His Letters*. His research interests include the epistle to the Hebrews, the use of the Old Testament in the New, the doctrine of the atonement, theological exegesis, Second Corinthians and the reception history of Exodus and Deuteronomy. He lives in Spokane with his wife, Annie, and their two children.

SUBJECT INDEX

Finding the Textbook You Need

The IVP Academic Textbook Selector
is an online tool for instantly finding the IVP books
suitable for over 250 courses across 24 disciplines.

ivpacademic.com